WORK
YOUR
Room

DR. DAVID E. JACKSON

ME
WE
PUBLISHING

Scripture references are taken from the King James Version of the
Holy Bible unless otherwise noted.
Pronouns for referring to the Father, Son and Holy Spirit are
capitalized intentionally and the words satan and devil are never
capitalized.

Publisher:
More Excellent Way Enterprises
www.mewellc.com

First Edition
ISBN: 978-0-9864235-5-0

Library of Congress Control Number: 2016910780

Printed in the United States of America.

I would like to dedicate this book to the memory of my late Grandmother, Mother Nancy Bee Taylor-Hankerson. I received my call to preach sitting on the front porch reading the Bible to you. You encouraged me to preach and sing as a child. You allowed me to play doctor on you and to share my dreams with you. You watched me grow every step of the way. I wish you were still here to read this book and witness this day. But I know you are a part of the great cloud of witnesses smiling from Heaven. I miss you and love you much.

TABLE OF CONTENTS

ACKNOWLEDGEMENTS

I give all the praise, glory, and honor to my Lord and Savior Jesus Christ who has given me the grace, skills, intellect, experiences, and strength to write this book.

I would like to thank my family for your constant support. To my Queen Mother, Dr. E. Taylor-Jackson: Thank you for believing in me when all the odds were against us. To my brother and his family: Elder Tavis Jackson, Lady Crystal Jackson, Brianna Jackson, and DaShuan Jackson for being a consistent support. To my deceased Father, the late Mr. David E. Jackson for providing fuel to make me want to overcome the odds. I am thankful to God for placing me in a prophetic priestly family. I love you all.

I thank God for my loving God parents and siblings: Rev. Dr. Kenneth and Rev Yolanda Clarke, Min. Ethan and Lady Fatima Bannister, and Mr. Kenny Clarke. Thank you for your constant declarations of support, love, and belief in my purpose.

I want to thank my staff at D.E. Jackson Enterprises, LLC: Elders Albert and Etoyi Billings, Pastor Leticia Douglas, Deacon Anthon and Eldress Cindy Bailey, Elder Tavis Jackson, and Eldress Eureka Mason. Without your hard work, prayers, sacrifices and support, this book would not be possible. May the goodly hands of the Almighty continue to prosper you in every way.

I am grateful for my Bishop and spiritual Mother, Dr. Ruth W. Smith for her genuine love and support. You are a blessing to me in ways I cannot express. Thank you so much for all that you have done and continue to do.

I honor the memory of my deceased Father in ministry, the late Archbishop Wilbert S. McKinley of the Elim International Fellowship, Brooklyn, NY. I will never forget our conversation in the car wherein you declared to me that I would be one of your sons that would write many books in your stead. Thank you so much your Grace for your impartation and instructions. Cush Arise and YADAH!

I salute the Mt. Sinai Baptist Church Family and the Light of the World Decatur Church for allowing me to serve as your Pastor and Overseer respectively. Thank you for your prayers, support and well-wishes.

I am appreciative of my supervisors, colleagues, and friends at the Atlanta Police Department. Your support and encouragement means so much to me.

To all the friends, colleagues, mentors, advisors, family members and supporters who remain nameless but are absolutely essential to the completion of this work, I say THANK YOU!

I send a big thank you and appreciation to Min. Charlotte Dudley and the More Excellent Way Enterprises, LLC for graciously taking on this project and making it a great success! Thank you so much and may God continue to bless you.

FOREWORD

It is with great joy that I share this foreword in support of Dr. Jackson, an anointed, intelligent, and articulate man of God. As you read this book, you will discover an undeniable revelation from the very mind of God. It is evident that Dr. Jackson understands the concept of "working your room" as he shares with you the many aspects of this process.

The core teaching of this book comes from Proverbs 18:16, *"A man's gift maketh room for him, and bringeth him before great men."* This principle is frequently portrayed in the pages of Scripture and helpfully expounded in this book by Dr. David Jackson. In fact, it is clearly illustrated throughout his own life.

I urge you to pay close attention to the three principles Dr. Jackson explains in Section I of this book. There is a vital connection between the gifts and calling of God in our lives. Unless we discern what God has given us, we can easily diminish the fantastic opportunities He has for us.

Our sense of direction depends on our understanding of God's purpose for our lives. All of God's children have unique gifts and callings from our heavenly Father. Those gifts are part of God's unchanging purpose for our lives. In fact, the Scripture tells us that the gifts and calling of the Lord are without repentance (See Romans 11:29). He does not change His mind about us. Although we may have only glimpses of his great purposes in our lives, He is still at work to bring them to fruition.

Even before his birth, John the Baptist was being fashioned for divine purpose where his gifts would point to the Lamb of God who takes away the sin of the world (See Luke 1:13-17). In Jeremiah 1:5, we see that God formed Jeremiah in his mother's womb and set him apart and ordained him a prophet to the nations.

I think of those in Scripture who were little children like Samuel when God first spoke to them about his plan (See 1 Samuel 3). Or, what about Joseph? As a young man, he had glimpsed God's purpose for him to serve in a position of extraordinary leadership, even over his family (See Genesis 37). In spite of unjust treatment and adverse circumstances, he continued to exercise his gifts in every way possible. Eventually, those gifts opened the door for him to become second in command of the most powerful nation on earth. Also, that role permitted him to spare his family, the patriarchs of the nation of Israel, from destruction. Without any question, Joseph's gifts made room for him in the palace of Pharaoh.

Do not imagine that God has no plan, no purpose, or no provision for your life. None of God's children have been deprived of the gifts necessary to fulfill his purpose in their lives (See 1 Corinthians 12:5-11). He may indeed have called you to do the impossible, but all things are possible with Him (See Matthew 19:26, Luke 18:27). With Him and His gifts, you can do everything He calls you to do (See Philippians 4:13). Regardless of the obstacles that might otherwise discourage us, the gifts God has given us are sufficient for our every need (See 2 Corinthians 3:5-6). He can use the humble, the uneducated, the weak, and the poor by giving them inner resources that overflow in outward blessings to the people of his kingdom (See 2 Corinthians 12:9, 1 Corinthians 1:20-31).

The sons and daughters of God often fulfill their destiny in ways they did not plan and hardly understood even as it was unfolding. Remember Queen Esther, whose beauty and grace drew the attention of a powerful king. God gave her the courage and compassion necessary to fulfill His redemptive purpose for the nation of Israel. She exercised her calling with full surrender to God, saying, "If I perish, I perish." God gave her the wisdom to prevail (See Esther 4-7).

It is common for people to draw boundaries around themselves. They imagine limitations based upon their human ability as if they have forgotten the gifts that God has often bestowed upon the helpless and humble. It is easy to focus on what we cannot do instead of relying on the God who can do all things. Even though you cannot do anything you want, you can do anything God wants you to do.

Dr. Jackson draws a distinction between our natural abilities and spiritual gifts. That is imperative for understanding how to "work you room." Until you recognize your spiritual gifts, you live with unshakable handicaps. Natural limitations seem invincible until you receive the supernatural enabling of God's Spirit.

Acts 13:36 tells us that only after David had fulfilled God's purpose in his own generation did he finally die. When Jesus Christ ascended into the heavens, this world still had many needs. It isn't that he had no concern about those who were still sick and suffering or no compassion for those who were poor and perishing. He left behind a body of people, his church. That church shook the world with the proclamation of good news confirmed by displays of God's power working through individual believers.

God has a purpose for you too, doesn't He? Along with that purpose, He has been at work in your life. He has provided you with a unique combination of natural and spiritual gifts. Unfortunately, many people focus all their attention on their natural abilities and resources. By failing to pursue spiritual gifts as commanded in first Corinthians 14, they ignore God's provision to enlarge their influence for His glory and their good. Dr. John Maxwell says, "When you find your spiritual gift, God will give you an opportunity to use it."

Although there are many spiritual gifts, they all come from one Source, the Spirit of God. Just as there is incredible unity among the persons of the Godhead, these gifts are intended to work together in perfect harmony. Some people receive gifts that attract lots of attention. The gifts of others are hardly noticed. However, every gift opens doors and makes room for greatness (See 1 Corinthians 12). True greatness is not found in the praise of man, but in serving others (See Matthew 23:11). God's spiritual gifts enable the least, the lowest, and the last among us to bring blessing into the lives of those who have lost hope.

As Charles Haddon Spurgeon said, "God never loses sight of the treasure which He has placed in our earthen vessels." I hope you have discovered the gifts God has deposited within you. If you have, this book will expand your perspective on how to exercise those gifts most effectively. If you haven't, I am excited for you. This book can help you find the gifts He has provided so that you can enlarge your impact according to His purpose.

Dr. Ruth W. Smith
Light of the World Interdenominational
International Association

PREFACE

When I was a young child, I had a strong sense of what I thought my purpose in life was supposed to be. There was an unstoppable and deep, abiding passion towards ministry and medicine inside my tiny heart. At the tender age of three, I started setting up my grandmother's coffee table as a pulpit in the center of the living room on Sunday afternoons. I would put her tattered King James Version family Bible on it, though I could not read then. Nonetheless, I would just open it up and allow the pages to rest on the place where it would land. On the couch across from the coffee table, would sit my wide variety of stuffed toys formed into a small congregation, with my younger brother, baby cousin, and Grandma in attendance. Soon after the stage was set up, random sounds from my grandfather's modest but lovely piano would ring throughout the house as I placed my fingers on the keys glaring at the Hymnal perched on the ledger. "Ma sang!" would belt out of my little mouth to my Grandma giving her the cue to sing a hymn such as "Just a Closer Walk with Thee." Then I would repeat verbatim what I had heard the preacher say at church.

Considering all the obstacles and challenges I had to face at an early age, this childhood experience was quite amazing and unprecedented. Why? Really, before I was even born into the world, there was a plot to stop my birth. My dear mother once told me a story of her life as a pregnant woman. While I was in her womb, she was passing through a very difficult time wherein she wanted to give up. By God's providence, my Mom came across a lady who advised her to consult with a woman of God in Florida. The lady did not know my mother, but she knew God. She declared to her, saying, "Hang in there because you are carrying a son and he will be great. He will be known around the world."

Fortunately, I came into this world, growing and growing in stature, but not without problems. I had to struggle with attack after attack that ranged from being diagnosed as mentally retarded at the age of three to fighting learning disabilities, severe stuttering, and delayed speech. How could a little, promising boy who could barely put a sentence together become a preacher and a doctor? My speech was so hard to understand that a speech therapist told my parents that there was no hope of me being able to speak clearly because of my race and religious background. My parents had a heated discussion in the process of making a decision based on the words of the child developmental specialist, who told my parents that I was severely mentally retarded and recommended that I be placed in an institution. Thankfully, my mother discerned my purpose in life, and then made a decision to provide me with all the support I would need to reach my destiny. Her determination coupled with the purpose I felt in my heart gave me the drive and tenacity to become what I saw in my dreams despite what reality—my physical conditions—constantly presented to me. Funny enough, despite my undying passion for preaching, I never considered it as a vocation, but a call; and my marketplace passion was medicine.

My chief aspiration was to become the first medical doctor in my family. My maternal aunt was a nurse at the largest hospital in Atlanta, GA, and my grandmother would take me there to see her often. I would become lost in a world of fascination each time I entered the lobby of the hospital. The sounds that buzzed from all directions, which came from various equipment, the ding of the elevator, and the colors that popped from the employees' scrubs all grabbed my attention. Along with these experiences, I also noticed that many of my family members had health challenges, and I wanted to do something about it. I would lay hands and pray for their healing as a kid, and they would be healed. However, I knew there was something more I could do to help them stay well and wanted to do what was necessary to achieve that.

Coincidentally, many of my Christmas gifts had something to do with health and medicine: play doctor kits, stethoscopes, and chemistry sets to name a few. I spent all of my schoolings preparing to become a physician who would preach on the side. Having this sense of my purpose at an early age was a powerful guiding force in my life. The decisions I made, things I paid attention to, and the places I wanted to explore were all connected to what I thought was supposed to be my God-given purpose. Moreover, this sense of purpose was so powerful that the painful, disappointing, and seemingly hindering experiences in my life were never strong enough to kill my destiny! I won the battle in my mind.

In all of this, I soon realized a vital truth to my life's journey. I came to the tough reality that what I thought was my purpose was not God's purpose for my life! Peradventure, my childhood instinct, and intuition made me believe something other than what God intended for me in the first place. I want to ask you a serious question as you read this book: Do you know your God-given purpose? The reality is that PURPOSE is powerful but only if you know what it is, and provided it is the same as what God intends. Your self-designed purpose will not prosper; only what God has determined and designed for you will yield sustainable results.

While finding and knowing our purpose is of great importance in today's society, many are unaware of their purpose. As I interact with numerous people in ministry and my marketplace assignments, I discover that a large number of them have no idea what their divine purpose is. Some have even said, "I am just going through life aimlessly." This is not the will of God for your life, beloved! The reality is that if you do not know your purpose, you are just in existence and not living life. You are more or less the living dead in town and sadly, to say, you are not alive if you do not know your purpose. But there is hope! If you are yet to uncover your real purpose, or you are not sure if what you have discovered is genuine, then this book is for you. If you are sure of your purpose but not walking in its fulfillment, then you surely want to keep reading too. I am confident of this fact about you: you are too valuable and important to God and the world to be unaware of your purpose and not fully operating in it!

A short but powerful quote says, "Time is of the essence." Knowing your purpose is more important than ever before because of the time and the season that we are in. You may be asking me, "What time and season is that?" I am referring to the End Times, which is the time that precedes the second coming of Jesus Christ to the Earth. Those who grew up in or are familiar with religious settings where they have heard this term "End Times" or "the Last Days" may be indifferent to hearing this again on the pages of this book. I can remember 30 years ago when my grandmother used to tell us, "We are living in the last and evil days." And so now 30 years later, countless others and I are looking around for the Lord Jesus to return, and He has not returned yet. Sad enough, most Christians, God's Kingdom ambassadors, hear the statement but no longer have the zeal, excitement, or urgency to live each day on purpose, because of purpose, and with purpose as the motivating force for living. I urge you today to reconsider your posture to End Times. It is much more than a phrase—it is a reality.

As we look around the world at the wars, rumors of wars, violence, breakdown in the family structure, and increasing ungodliness in this society, we see that the Lord's return is imminent and closer than we may think. Therefore, for Kingdom people, this means that knowing your purpose, finding your purpose, and getting involved in your purpose is more important than it has ever been. We do not have time to play games and as such, we have to be serious, intentional, focused, and constantly moving towards that great destiny that lies in Eternity. With all of this said, I think what is even more alarming than a Kingdom person not knowing his/her purpose is for the individual to know it but not pursue it, let alone discover the specific aspect that offers him/her a greater experience of progress, success, and opportunities.

You might have landed safely and effectively in the place of your purpose but do you know how you got there? By chance, you just happened to find yourself in the place or position you are now…the place you have been waiting for, but you have no idea how you got there. To me, that is more problematic than not knowing your purpose. My point of this argument is that if you do not know the mechanics of how you found success in purpose, then that means you cannot reproduce success with confidence. When you know the power of your purpose and how that purpose achieved success, then you can do it over and over without any hassle, and you can even train others in that light. If you are just progressing without the knowledge of how and why, then your future efforts to recreate prosperity will be a hit-and-miss effort at best.

Even as I have looked at my life today, I realize that I did not land in purpose by accident. My ability to discern and embrace my purpose at a young age also gave me the ability to know the different aspects of my gifting and abilities. Over the years, this knowledge has enabled me, by God's grace, to make wise and strategic moves, adjustments, and decisions. While I did not become a medical doctor, I am in the center of my purpose. My journey has taken me on many twists and turns, some unexpected and many foreseen. Yet, at every turn, the burning passion I had developed at childhood gave me the ability to overcome numerous challenges and today, I am a witness and a testimony of the power of purpose.

I glory in God today that I am serving as the senior pastor of a growing multigenerational, historic church in downtown Atlanta with overseer duties as a young bishop in an association that provides leadership and ministerial coverage to over 250,000 people in 13 nations. I have a bright marketplace assignment as a Law Enforcement professional with a triple capacity: community affairs, chaplaincy, and adjunct instruction at the police academy. Lastly, I am the president and CEO of a thriving enterprise providing consultancy and training in church security, church growth, and educational development. Again, I share this not to brag about my abilities. I share this with you because as I have reflected on my journey, I have learned some principles and strategies that have assisted me in not only achieving success, but also in reproducing success when having to start over. I must be honest and transparent in saying that I have had to rebuild my life a few times. However, by God's grace, it did not take me long to rebuild and surpass my previous place because I have developed a blueprint based upon eight Kingdom principles that I have learned through my life experience.

The purpose of this book is to share with you these principles. First, allow me to share with you how this book was birthed. At the end of last year, one of my Elders—who is like an aunt to me—asked me to speak on the Power of Purpose at a Family and Marketplace Summit. As I began to pray and seek direction from God about the topic, the Holy Spirit directed me to a familiar passage of scripture in Proverbs 18:16 NKJV, *"A man's gift makes room for him, and brings him before great men."*

This scripture has been one of my favorites for most of my adult life as I have worked to be intentional and live on purpose. As I began to study this passage more closely, God allowed me to see that my entire life's journey towards fulfilling my God-given purpose had been governed by the three parts of this verse: gifts, room, and great people.

You may be asking, "What does purpose have to do with Proverbs 18:16?" To understand your purpose, you must know that purpose is directly linked to your gifts, both natural and spiritual. If you do not know your gifts, then you would never know and fully understand your purpose. One night as I lay down to sleep, I heard "Work Your Room!" in my spirit. I sat up and asked, "Lord, what do you mean?" I heard Him again, saying, "People are always asking me for opportunities to advance, opened doors to prosper, and resources to succeed but they fail to recognize that I have already given them the gifts, placed them in the room, and surrounded them with the people they need to fulfill their purpose!" I was so overwhelmed by this statement that I could not sleep for the rest of the night. From a series of divine encounters, Work Your Room was birthed. Allow me to be your coach and walk with you through this book as I share life-giving, transforming Kingdom principles that will literally activate and move you into your divine destiny in a way you only imagined.

Work Your Room presents eight Kingdom principles in three sections. Section I is based upon the first part of Proverbs 18:16, which deals with knowing your gift. As I stated earlier, to understand your purpose, you must know your gifts. I will discuss God's intent in giving us special abilities and talents and how to find the intersection between your natural abilities and spiritual gifts. Section I will, therefore, present the first three principles. Principle 1 is "Purpose Gives Direction." This principle will show you that purpose provides a roadmap for each step in your journey. Kingdom people who desire to have a life that is filled with destiny and purpose must pattern their lives according to that purpose—and should not engage in anything that would not promote their God-given purpose. Principle 2 is "Discovering and Prioritizing Your Gift Increases Your Value." Once you figure out what your gifts are, then you can take the next important step of placing your gifts in order of priority. Some factors generally influence the degree of importance you can assign to each gift or talent. Your ability to recognize the gifts that should be your dominant ones will position you in such a way as to increase your value to people around you. Principle 3 is "Determining the Value of your Gift Directly Affects Your Demand Level." Once you have prioritized your gifts to a state where they are and can be valued, now you are in a place where people, places, and things want you to bring your gift to the table. What is the point of having a gift if it is not in demand?

From here, we will journey to Section II, "Recognizing that You are in Your Room." Proverbs 18:16 says that your gifts will make room for you. In this section, I will share why it is important to recognize that you are in your room. Also, we will discuss how to recognize that you are in your room and how to manage or handle your room. In Section II, we will discuss Principles 4, 5, and 6. Principle 4 is "Acknowledging Your Moment is Equally Important to Knowing Your Gift." This is so vital because if you know your gift without recognizing that you are in your room or moment, then you will be in your room but be impotent. Principle 5 is "Keep the Old and New in Proper Perspective." One of the biggest enemies to purpose is using old methods and strategies in a new place. This principle shows that you have to make the proper transition in order to work your room. Principle 6 is "Preparation Starts before the Room, Not in the Room." This principle is absolutely essential to working your room because your commitment to preparation will affect the timing of reaching the place wherein purpose is manifested. Your lack of preparation can also hinder your performance in your room.

Next, we will explore Section III, "Engaging Great People." Yes, your gifts will make room for you; but it does not stop there. Your gifts, being put in proper operation and perspective, will also bring you before great people. Working with and in front of great people requires skills beyond your gifting. This is often where many Kingdom people "drop the ball" in the area of purpose. I will share tools to help you maximize your moment and optimize the resources you now have in the people that surround you, to make sure you succeed exceedingly. Section III will explore Principles 7 and 8. Principle 7 is "Great People only Entertain Great People so Act like It!" This is so true beloved. If your gifts and personality were not great, then you would not have an audience with great people. Although it can be intimidating and nerve-racking to be in a new place of divine connection with amazing people, you need the confidence and "swag" to manage these new and crucial relationships. Principle 8 is "Management of Your Inner Life is Essential to Surviving the Politics Attached to Great People." While being connected to great people is amazing, it comes with some politics. There are people who will be in the room with you but do not want you there, nor do they want you to succeed. Great people often have blind spots or tunnel vision and may overlook (by choice or by accident) some of the dynamics going on in the room. What is sure is that they are willing to invest in you and to give you a chance to work your room. However, if you do not get a handle on your insecurities and other related issues, you will destroy your own moment.

We will close out this journey together with "You Made it to the Room BUT do not Get too Comfortable!" In the postlude, I will encourage you to keep what is happening in your life in proper perspective. Achieving success is wonderful and exciting, but unless you have reached your resting place (I will discuss this later), then you should monitor or watch out for the possibility of getting satisfied where you are. Contentment is necessary, but ambition is key. Get ready for an exciting journey into Working Your Room. I want to start this trip with you by stating that my staff and I have prayed, fasted, and worshipped over this material to ensure that as you read this book, you will receive an impartation of wisdom, strategy, faith, and grace, so that you can fully become all that God has preordained for you before the world began. Without further ado, get ready to WORK YOUR ROOM!

Dr. David E. Jackson

SECTION I

Knowing Your Gift

"A man's gift…" (Psalm 18:16)

The value of your life is a function of your measure of knowledge, and knowledge, as they say, is power—the ability to perform, to deliver. Therefore, your breakthrough in life starts with knowing who you are, and your identity is largely tied to the talent you have. More so, your gift is your means to success, happiness, and fulfillment.

The focus scripture for this book again is Proverbs 18:16, which says, "A man's gift makes room for him, and brings him before great men." This is an important concept that you must not only know but also sincerely believe and embrace. If you were honest right now, you would admit that you have gone through some things in life that made you feel like you had nothing of value to offer. On the contrary, early in your life while growing up, you may be the only one who knew you were valuable but have had to fight hard to get above all the obstacles and haters along the way. You probably had self-inspired support and encouragement to be all that you could be, but now, you are at a crossroads in life and are feeling a little stuck and stagnant. Regardless of where you fall in the purpose spectrum, you must know and believe that you have a gift that God has bestowed on you, which is directly connected to your purpose and moment. This moment includes people that will provide you with the necessary resources to push you even further into your destiny. This is why you cannot afford to despise "little things" in your journey in life. Yes, for instance, the hurtful, painful, embarrassing, and uncomfortable things that have happened to you have been quite necessary to you being who you are today. They were required to shape and design the gifts in you. Oftentimes, because of the experiences we have had, we lose sight of the reason for everything and become heavy with the "whys" of the journey. When we focus on "why me," then we can misjudge our journey and then overlook the gifts that God has placed inside us.

Do Not Misjudge Your Journey

Again, I ask you, "Have you misjudged your journey?" I raise it again because having the wrong perspective on your life and your present state—where you are—can blind you to your purpose. When you are blind to your purpose, then you will miss or overlook the valuable lessons that life is trying to teach you so that you can possess your destiny. Nonetheless, sometimes, you can feel that you are wasting time because you may not be where you want to be. You may feel like you are on a pointless, time-wasting mission like Saul, the son of Kish, felt when he went searching his father's donkeys.

And Samuel answered Saul, and said, I am the seer: go up before me unto the high place; for ye shall eat with me to day, and to morrow I will let thee go, and will tell thee all that is in thine heart. And as for thine asses that were lost three days ago, set not thy mind on them; for they are found. And on whom is all the desire of Israel? Is it not on thee, and on all thy father's house? And Saul answered and said, Am not I a Benjamite, of the smallest of the tribes of Israel? and my family the least of all the families of the tribe of Benjamin? wherefore then speakest thou so to me? (1 Samuel 9:19-21)

Yes, to most people, life can feel like a task that seems to have no connection to their purpose because it is sometimes filled with 'donkey chases.' What is a donkey chase? A donkey chase is an experience that on the surface has no direct connection to your destiny or desired place of personal fulfillment. When I was in school, I used to get some assignments from my teachers that were important to my education as they were required for me to pass the class. But sometimes, especially on days we had substitute teachers, we would get some "busy work." These assignments had nothing to do with what we had been studying nor were they necessary to pass the class. It was simply to keep us busy, just to pass away the time. That is how donkey chases feel at first. But if I had looked deeper and closer, I would realize that I was being given a golden substance wrapped up in a rag. That suggests to me that opportunities do not always come in a nice-looking package. If you are chosen and destined for greatness, then NOTHING—and I mean NOTHING—that happens in your life comes by accident or without a purpose. Even the things that seem to have no direct link to your purpose and assignment in life has value. It is all a matter of perspective.

The very experience you seem to underrate or complain about right now may be the machinery that is going to push you directly into your moment. So if you give up now, you will forfeit your one-time opportunity to step into the realm of fulfillment. Saul's donkey chase led him on a journey that his heart only dreamed of: becoming the leader of his people. Without this seemingly useless task, Saul would have remained stuck in a hopeful wish. Every step and part of your journey is ordained to get you closer to your moment! If you have the wrong attitude and posture about your life experiences, you will delay the manifestation of your destiny. The reality is that you may be closer to your next level than you think or feel but you may be far from experiencing it

[4]

because of poor attitude and perspective about your current engagements, circumstances, experience, or state of life. What a shame it would be to have come this far on your life's journey and then miss your moment because of wrong perspective and a negative outlook. Examine your viewpoint on life and make a decision to see the glass of life as "half full" and not "half empty." Be optimistic, hopeful, and ambitious rather than being pessimistic, hopeless, and lethargic. God is about to shift your life faster and sooner than you think. I pray that you will not miss your time but be ready to enter into your purpose. In order to maintain this positive outlook, you have to accept that on your journey to discovering your God-given purpose and gifts, you will make tons of mistakes. There will be missteps, toxic connections, and unavoidable blunders on your journey to destiny. However, despite all of the mistakes you might make, rest assured that they cannot cancel out your ultimate God-given destiny. In fact, the mistakes have been factored into the equation. My friend, do not allow mistakes to make you a prisoner of your past but use it as a tool to learn more about your gifts and purpose.

Factored In

Making mistakes in life is as normal as walking and breathing. We are human, and it is given that we will mess up on a regular basis. Many people, however, allow past mistakes and errors to keep them in chains of shame and regret. The consequences of the past may very well be felt, seen, or known in your present and could linger into your future. Nonetheless, recognize that despite your past mistakes and their consequences, you are still making movement towards your purpose and destiny. I want to challenge you to look at your past mistakes differently. Sometimes, you can look back and say, "I wish I had not done this or that," or wonder, "How would my life be if I had not done this or if I had not missed that moment?" The reality is that you would not be who you are today if you had not gone through EVERY thing you have. Look at it this way: God FACTORED every experience you have had, including the mistakes, INTO your journey! Psalm 37:23 states that, "The steps of a good man are ordered by the LORD; and He delights in his way." The Apostle Paul declares in his letter to the church at Rome, saying, *"We know that all things work together for good for those who love God, to those who are the called according to His purpose"* (Romans 8:28).

To Kingdom people, nothing that has happened has been by accident or by happenstance. This means that even the mess-ups, errors, mistakes, missed opportunities, hardships, and struggles cannot stop or hinder the ultimate purpose and destiny set out for your life, for they are all part of the process or equation. This is why the Scriptures say that in everything we are to give THANKS, for this is God's will for us (1 Thessalonians 5:18).

Your mistakes will not hinder you from reaching your future but will rather shape you for your destiny if you learn the lessons the mistakes taught you. Do not allow your emotions, thoughts, or people to make you feel hopeless and trapped by your past. Recalibrate your perspective and embrace all that you have experienced with the understanding that you are destined to win, and NOTHING is going to stop you, NOT EVEN YOUR MISTAKES. Why? It is because they were already factored into the journey. Keep on walking the path, because you are closer to destiny than you think.

Gifts Are Clues in Life

The path of life that we find ourselves on often gives us clues and indicators to where we are supposed to be headed and how we are to get there. One of the most important clues in life is your gifts. What are gifts? Gifts are both natural and spiritual abilities and talents that God has invested in you so you can be someone—a role player—in His overall plan, and do a predetermined assignment in this world. Gifts come in wide varieties, both small and great. Irrespective of its size, so to say, a gift is a gift. Gifts can include your lovely singing voice, ability to make amazing desserts from scratch, giving great attention to detail and organizational skills, and compassion that leads you to feed the hungry and clothe the naked. Your ability to pray for extended periods and stand in the gap for those who have burdens and are seeking divine solutions is a special gift many people have. The list can go on and on. The reality is that every person walking on the face of the earth has a gift and talent. However, several would tell you, if asked, that they do not have a gift or talent. This belief is not true in any form or fashion. The fact that you are breathing and reading this book is proof that you have something on the inside of you, which is of great importance and value. It is amazing how life experiences, be it abuse, neglect, or struggle, can cause some people to devalue, belittle or ignore the gifts and talents they possess. Others have taken advantage of the challenging experiences of life and used them as their motivation to defy the odds and make a liar out of every naysayer.

Regardless of where you fall, I want to remind you and affirm that you have something of great importance and value inside you. I do not care about what was told to you, what has happened to you, or what you have gone through—you are too gifted to be a nonentity in this world. Lay your hand on your chest and take a good look in the mirror and say, "I have something of great importance and value inside me." You may think that this is pointless or crazy, but I beg to differ. You will never come into the full discovery of your gifts until you first acknowledge, admit, and accept that you have gifts that were placed inside you for the betterment of the world. Even more powerful than this is that only YOU can do what YOU can do the way that YOU do it! You are a unique bundle of divine purpose waiting to be unwrapped and manifested. I love that! I love it because it takes the pressure off your life as to you trying to be someone else. So you do not have to compare yourself to other people, even if they have the same gifts and talents. You are uniquely made and fashioned by the Creator and birthed into the world for such a time as this so that you can make your authentic contribution to humanity. In order to make your unique mark on the world, you have to find out why you are here.

Why are you alive and breathing? You are not alive to just pay bills and just go through the same experiences year in and year out. You were created for so much more than that. Bishop TD Jakes, first class Kingdom and business mogul, says it best, "Knowing God's divine purpose in your life is one of the greatest assets and enablements to help understand and make sense of the perplexities and complications that seem to overwhelm. People who possess such knowledge possess power." To come to the full manifestation of the essence—purpose—of your existence, you have to know without question and with total confidence what God Almighty has deposited on the inside of you.

Discovering Your Gifts

As stated earlier on, gifts include both natural and spiritual abilities. Why do I discuss both natural and spiritual gifts? I do so because some people like to emphasize the spiritual part of their gifts and ignore or devalue the natural ones. We should not forsake or overlook the natural aspect of our gifts. This is important because separating your natural abilities from your spiritual talent would amount to walking in partial ignorance of who you are. The late Dr. Myles Monroe, a leading Kingdom and Marketplace leader, said, "The greatest enemy of man is ignorance of self. Nothing is more frustrating than not knowing who you are or what to do with what you have." Let me take a step further. I want to encourage you not only to discover what your natural and spiritual gifts are but also to find the link or connection between your natural and spiritual gifts. The wisdom of this age is to find the intersection or the nexus of your natural and spiritual gifts and resist the urge to separate or place them in different boxes as though they were designed never to touch each other. How do you find the connection? You have to figure out what makes your natural and spiritual gifts connect. At what point do they overlap or are similar? I knew very early in life that I had a natural ability for expressing my thoughts and opinion—I was very outspoken and bold. Sometimes, I was too good at it and would find myself in a world of trouble for being so direct and honest. However, as I got older and accepted Jesus as my Lord and Savior, I was able to connect my natural ability to communicate with my calling to preach and the associated spiritual gifts that enhanced my ability to share God's heart and mind with people, in and outside the church. I knew that the gift of communication, be it in the marketplace or the church, would be much more effective and persuasive if I linked up my natural and spiritual gifts.

Find the Nexus of Your Gifts

What I love about God in relation to finding the nexus of gifts is that He knows how to endow you with the right mixture of natural and spiritual abilities to make a winning combination in your life. The work of figuring out how to pair what with what and where to play it out can be the challenging part. But if you open your eyes and pay attention to what your life's experiences are trying to teach you through the challenges, opposition, and opportunities presented to you, then you will start to see the overlapping space that your spiritual and natural gifts can create for your benefit. I have both a marketplace and a religious, Kingdom mandate. My marketplace assignment is in law enforcement and government while my religious work is serving as a senior pastor of a thriving multigenerational church and as a young bishop in an international association of churches and ministries. I never forget one day, I was in my office reading an article about an incident that happened at a local church. The elderly receptionist of the church allowed a young man to come into the church during a weekday to use the phone. Unfortunately, the lady was at the church alone, and the juvenile attacked the woman and took her possessions. This story connected to dozens more that I was familiar with when it came to crimes against places of worship and their adherents. I heard a voice inside say, "You can do something about it, you know!" Instantly, a light bulb went on in my head—I can create a Church security training to better equip faith leaders on how to secure their property and protect members and visitors from crimes and terrorism. From this was birthed my seminar that I have conducted in many churches in the last few years. The book and the work manual for this training will be published later this year, and I am always excited to offer the teaching to congregations across the US. I share this because it shows that I was able to find the connection between my natural gift, which manifests in my secular/marketplace assignment, and my spiritual endowment, which equips me in my church/Kingdom role. I want to equip you to do same, and as well help you to find success in your life by discovering and utilizing your spiritual and natural gifts.

By connecting your natural and spiritual abilities in meaningful ways, you will eventually position yourself to be valued and paid for doing what you were created to do and not just work a job or have a career doing what pays the bills only. Is that not the real heart cry of many Kingdom people today? To make money doing the thing that they were born to do! If you do not recognize the design and full composition of your gifts, spiritually and naturally, then you can end up making someone else wealthy and fulfilled while you feel frustrated, hopeless, and out of sync with your destiny. It is my prayer that as you continue to read this book, something will click inside of your mind, heart, and spirit and drive you to the total discovery of your personal purpose.

Natural Abilities

You may be asking, "Well, how do you find out what your gifts are?" Regarding your natural abilities, they are those things that you have always had inside of you as long as you can remember. I remember as a child that I had a natural ability of perceiving situations. I knew what was going on around with people even though, at that tender age, I did not have the intellectual and experiential capacity to know what was going on. I knew it intuitively. It would scare my parents and other adults around me because I would often blurt out things that I "knew" but was not supposed to know since I was still a child. As you can imagine, this got me in trouble at times and was even hated and rejected by some relatives. I did not know where it came from; it was just there! It has ALWAYS been a part of me and who I was.

Ask yourself these questions: What comes naturally to you? What comes easy, seamless, and endurable to you? Let me ask it another way, what would you do for free even though it is worth the money? Do not miss that part! Natural gifts are not just what you would do for free but are something so valuable and needed in the world that you deserve financial compensation. Therefore, if you are working or doing something without compensation or even if you are being paid, and yet you hate it, then it may not be in line with your purpose. However, if you can do it without getting a dime and feel totally fulfilled by doing it, then perhaps you are using your gifts in a way that aligns with purpose.

Here is another way to find your gifts: What problems do you automatically recognize and naturally develop strategies to solve? The reality is that there is something that bothers us all the time! But the things that may grab your attention may not even "phase" your family or friends. I want to challenge you not to overlook these things. Therein lies a clue or indication to what your natural abilities are and the way you can make a definite impact on the world. If you can discipline yourself to move past your irritation with the problem or situation and start asking yourself the right questions about the circumstance, you will uncover excellent opportunities. You may stumble upon an invention, start a business that offers strategies to potential clients, build a platform to spread your beliefs on the matter, or create a new association that gathers people of like minds to solve the issue with you. One last thing—your natural gifts will make you a problem-solver in the world.

Spiritual Gifts

When I was six, I made the conscious decision to accept Jesus as my Lord and Savior, but it was at the age of twelve that I allowed the Holy Spirit to fill me with His full presence. When I received Jesus as my Lord and Savior, God deposited spiritual gifts inside of me. This is the reality of all those who believe in Jesus. In the Bible, there are over 20 gifts mentioned in both the Old and New Testaments. Some of these gifts are administration, mercy, giving, prophecy, and exhortation. Some great places to start reading the Scriptures about spiritual gifts are Romans 12:6-8, 1 Corinthians 12:8-10, 28-30, and Ephesians 4:11. I have taught on spiritual gifts for over a decade now around the world. One of the things I teach is that the term "spiritual gift," in its original sense, comes from the Greek word charismata, which means grace or ability given directly from God. Therefore, the spiritual gifts that the Holy Spirit gives you at salvation are a result of God's grace extended towards you! Grace, in this context, means that God has given you good, useful, and powerful gifts/abilities not because you deserve it or did something to earn it. On the contrary, these gifts have been given to you because of the love that God has for you and to fulfill His ultimate purpose in your life.

This fact overwhelms my heart to the point of tears sometimes! When I think of how flawed and inconsistent I am in my humanity, I am amazed that God overlooked all of this and still gave me powerful and effective spiritual abilities. My sins, weaknesses, and proclivities did not revoke the transfer of His grace gifts into my life. I do not know about you, but I am so grateful and humbled by this understanding. That is why when I changed from my life's pursuit from medicine to ministry, I willingly obeyed God's directive. During this time, I also discovered, at a deeper level, the spiritual gifts God had given me despite my mess! Besides, I had a lot of problems and issues going on during my early twenties. Nevertheless, none of that stopped God from using me greatly for His glory. The same applies to you, beloved! Despite your addiction, your secrets, or your mistakes, if you are a believer in Jesus Christ as Lord, then these things did not disqualify you from receiving spiritual gifts! If anything, it is your journey and struggles that will provide the breeding ground for your spiritual gifts to be manifested even the more. It will also allow people to know without any doubt that your abilities did not come from you, but they came from God. Paul the Apostles says, *"But we have this treasure in earthen vessels, that the excellency of the power may be of God, and not of us"* (2 Corinthians 4:7).

Spiritual Gifts Assessments

A useful way to find out what your spiritual gifts are is to a take spiritual gifts assessment. This is a series of questions that are designed to find out what your interests are, what draws your attention in the church/ministry, and how you have been endowed for service in God's Kingdom.

There are tons of assessments out there. Allow me to recommend a great online assessment tool I used with my ministers and church regularly at http://www.spiritualgiftstest.com/test/adult. This site will provide you with your top gifts as well as a thorough description of what each gift means. This information will be critical to your journey of purpose as you find out what your gifts are because once you discover them, you can then find out where your gifts can best be used in a local church and the world. I encourage my congregation to pay close attention to their primary, secondary, and tertiary (third level) gifts. From here, you can see what areas of the church these gifts will thrive in. For instance, if you have the gift of mercy, then you may be a good fit in your benevolence ministry or outreach team. Similarly, with the gift of exhortation, visiting the sick or the bereaved may be a wonderful avenue to meet people's needs for comfort and hope. Once you know your gifts, begin to maximize them by getting involved in a church or ministry that will allow you to use your gifts to the glory of God. Educate yourself as much as possible by reading articles, books, or attending seminars on the areas of your gifts.

When it comes to ministerial leaders, I usually challenge them to not only pay attention to their top three gifts in general but also pay attention to their top three of the five-fold ministry gifts described in Ephesians 4:11 — Apostle, Prophet, Evangelist, Pastor, and Teacher. The reason for saying this is that knowing your five-fold ministry gifts will direct you as to how your leadership in the church is best exercised. Did you know that many ministers are misplaced in the church? Without doubts, they are truly called of God to serve as licensed or ordained ministers, but they are still depressed or unmotivated because they are not doing what they believe or feel they were created to do. Knowing your five-fold gifts and then getting active in those areas will fulfill you in ways that will blow your mind. That fulfillment will bring joy as you can now activate what has been deposited on the inside of you and manifest it in powerful ways in the earth realm. At the end of the day, you have the gracious power and the ability to get consistent, effective, and resounding results in what you do. Purpose gives you motivation, and then power is released for action. If you lack power, you will not make headway in life. Perhaps that is why your ministry, business, or endeavor has been going on for years, and you are still not able to get the results you want. Maybe you are out of purpose, and you have no power; therefore, you are not getting any results. But you do not have to stay powerless. Discovering your spiritual gifts and using them in the appropriate area of ministry will release love, joy, and peace in your life in ways that only the Holy Spirit could give.

Marketplace and Kingdom Partnerships

With that said, I want to implore you to invest your time and energy into assignments, careers, and opportunities that truly align with your purpose and utilize both your natural and spiritual abilities. Three of the ways you will know this is happening are as follows: those you serve treat you with honor and respect; you are being compensated consistently and appropriately; and you get consistent results that can be duplicated.

Let me tell you this: stop walking around doing everything for free. You need to monetize your gifts or else you are going to be a broke and frustrated Kingdom person. I must tell you that "broke and Kingdom" is a paradox, and they do not go together. Perhaps, you might take offense at my statement because you do not want to link purpose, gifts, and money together—but I have to tell you the truth. God wants His people to experience prosperity in their purpose.

Prosperity is not all about money alone, but finance is an important feature of success. I mentioned earlier that you must find the nexus of your natural and spiritual gifts, and that finding this connection is linked to seeing how your marketplace and kingdom assignments align. As great as spiritual gifts are to the work of the ministry and the advancement of the Kingdom of God, we must branch out of the four walls of the church and ministry and reclaim our marketplace assignments. A marketplace assignment is basically what you do secularly or outside the church ministry/stewardship. Let us reiterate that a connection exists between your natural and spiritual gifts. Many times, our natural gifts play out in our secular vocation or marketplace assignment. Similarly, our spiritual gifts operate in our church or ministry tasks. I want to state categorically that God wants you to see both your secular and church work as KINGDOM WORK! Do not limit the Kingdom to what you do at church or in your ministry. Your Kingdom assignment includes what you do in your corporate setting as well as what you do at your church. Just as all Kingdom people are given spiritual gifts and a purpose to fulfill in the church, they are also called to conquer and dominate in one of the seven cultural mountains or spheres of society. These cultural mountains are Arts and Entertainment, Business, Education, Family, Government, Media, and Religion. If you are unfamiliar with this concept of cultural mountains or spheres, there are some great resources available online for you to explore and learn new things on how you can maximize your gifts in the secular world. Research and educate yourself on this notion. In so doing, you will have one foot in your marketplace mountain and then one foot in your church assignment, and then you will be a Kingdom force to be reckoned with. I thank God that

I stand in the mountain of Government and the mountain of Religion at the same time. Stand tall as a spiritual giant and fulfill the God-given destiny He gave you through the combination of both your spiritual and natural gifts. Do not allow challenges, lack of money, education, or limited connections to stop you from going after your purpose.

The Principles of Section I

In Section I, I would like to share three powerful principles that have helped me find success in my purpose as it relates to knowing my gifts. Principle 1 is "Purpose Gives Direction." This principle will show us that purpose provides a roadmap for each step in our journey. Kingdom people who desire to have a life that is filled with destiny and purpose must pattern their lives according to that purpose—and should not engage in anything that would not promote their God-given purpose. Principle 2 is "Discovering and Prioritizing Your Gift Increases Your Value." Once you figure out what your gifts are, then you can take the next important step of placing your gifts in order of priority. Some factors generally influence the degree of importance you can assign to each gift or talent. Your ability to recognize the gifts that should be your dominant ones will position you in such a way as to increase your value to people around you. Principle 3 is "Determining the Value of your Gift Directly Affects Your Demand Level." Once you have prioritized your gifts to a state where they are and can be valued, now you are in a place where people, places, and things want you to bring your gift to the table. What is the point of having a gift if it is not in demand?

PRINCIPLE 1

Purpose Gives Direction

Have you ever found yourself staring at the ceiling in your room wondering why you were awake when you should be sleeping? You might have gotten up and walked around your house, hoping to get sleepy enough so you could go back to sleep. Yet it seems not to work. Then a bright idea comes to mind to take a midnight stroll or drive to clear your mind since walking around the house is not working. You jump in your car and start driving around your neighborhood. You do not have a particular destination or a set of directions in mind. All you want is to clear your mind and heart of whatever is bogging it down.

While this exercise of driving around aimlessly might work in this instance, we cannot expect to make significant moves in our life towards destiny if we spend the majority of our time driving or walking around without a clear sense of direction. This is why knowing your purpose is quite vital to your existence.

Without purpose, you lack direction for your life and when you lack direction, you can find yourself wasting precious time on irrelevant or trivial things. Remember, your time is your life. Purpose gives you vision and it gives a good meaning to your life. In Proverbs 29:18, it clearly states that, "Where there is no vision, the people perish: but he that keepeth the law, happy is he."

While I appreciate the good ole King James Version, I also want you to see how the New International Version, the

New Living Translation, and the English Standard Version unpacks the true meaning of this verse:

New International Version:

"Where there is no revelation, people cast off restraint; but blessed is the one who heeds wisdom's instruction."

New Living Translation:

"When people do not accept divine guidance, they run wild. But whoever obeys the law is joyful."

English Standard Version:

"Where there is no prophetic vision, the people cast off restraint, but blessed is he who keeps the law."

So having a prophetic revelatory vision about your future gives you RESTRAINTS! Restraints are designed to set boundaries, give parameters, and lock you into place. Otherwise, you will run wild and all over the place. You cannot achieve success by being wild, undisciplined, and without direction. But getting a clear sense of direction from God as to why you are alive will streamline, discipline, settle, and govern you and all that you do. This is a challenging concept for many to embrace in light of YOLO (you only live once) philosophy which encourages people to do what they want to, how they want to, where they want to do it, and with whomever they choose to do it.

Having this type of mentality is also detrimental and often times contradictory to what God has for your life. Is it really worth it to do what pleases you, only to find that you have wasted so many precious years? This is why being governed by vision and not self-pleasure is a vital part to success in life.

Pattern Your Life after Vision

My father in ministry, the Late Bishop Wilbert McKinley, used to say that people of purpose must pattern their life after vision. This means that every decision you make in life must be strategic, well thought out, and in total alignment with the vision God has given you. That plays out in areas you may not readily think it would be necessary such as your location, your career choice, and your appearance. One key area to consider here is who you connect yourself to in relationship. When I say relationship, I mean all types of relationships, be it romantic, platonic, professional or familial. This is important because in order for a healthy relationship to exist, there must be partnership and agreement. The Bible says in Amos 3:3, "Can two walk together, except they be agreed?" With that said, how can you claim you are walking in agreement with someone who does not have the same vision as you? What true connection can you maintain in a healthy way with someone who does not believe in your purpose and destiny? Our connections with people influence our behaviors, our language, and our perspective on life—three critical aspects for attaining success in your purpose. Surrounding yourself with negative people or people with a narrow view of life can hinder you in ways you cannot imagine. Sometimes, things are being withheld or shaken in your life because of who you are connected to.

We see this plainly as day itself in the Book of Jonah. God came to him and told him to go and preach repentance at Nineveh. That was Jonah's purpose and destiny in God's plan of salvation. Jonah did not want to do that because he did not

[21]

want Gentiles to experience conversion and the same blessings that God's chosen people were enjoying. So he did what many people do when they do not want to do what God says, "RUN!" Jonah went in the complete opposite direction when he got on a ship heading to Tarshish instead of Nineveh. While he was in the bottom part of the boat sleeping, God began to shake the boat, tossing it to get Jonah's attention. But because he was asleep, he was not the one who was being negatively affected. No, it was other people on the ship, who were perhaps in alignment with their purpose. But because one person on the boat was out of purpose, even though he was loosely connected to them, their lives were threatened. Who is rocking your boat? Better still, whose boat are you rocking and do not even know it because you are wrongly connected? Vision must be the belt or strap that locks you into your purpose so that you will not be thrown off track by the various detours and distractions that will come on your journey. One of the biggest distractions can be your own self and desires.

Receive God's Blueprint and Abandon Yours

One of the challenges with people finding their purpose is that they have decided on their own what they want their purpose to be, with no thought of asking the Divine Creator why they were placed here—on Earth. We develop plans, make major decisions, and invest countless funds and time into our own ways often to see our plans fall completely apart in front of our very eyes. Proverbs 3:5-6 says, *"Trust in the Lord with all your heart, and lean not on your own understanding; In all your ways acknowledge Him, And He shall direct your paths."* Saul of Tarsus who later became Paul could relate to this. In the book of Acts, Saul was building a bright future for himself in the Sanhedrin, which was the religious-political system of Israel during the Roman Empire. Saul was wealthy, highly educated (he went to the Hillel, which was the Ivy League of his time and was taught directly by the great scholar Gamaliel) and a Jewish man with Roman citizenship. He made it his purpose to maintain the strength of Jewish faith in the midst of this new but growing faith in a man named Jesus of Nazareth. Saul sincerely felt that it was his life's purpose to persecute this group of believers that were called "Christians" first at Antioch. And he was very successful at his supposed "purpose." Some scholars would agree that Saul was responsible for the stoning of Deacon Stephen in Acts 6. However, Saul's entire life was transformed on the road to Damascus while he was fulfilling what he thought was his purpose. But Jesus encountered him and shifted the entire direction of Saul's life. As he was riding on his beast, he was suddenly knocked to the ground and blinded as a loud voice, beaming down from the sky in a bright beam of light, asked Saul the reason for persecuting Him. Has life ever knocked you down, and caused you to be blind to where you were and where you were going? Have you had life ask you the question of purpose and motive? Why are you doing this? You may think it is your life's purpose but may discover that you are actually fighting against your purpose. What a tough feeling to have thought that all of your efforts up to a certain point were in line with your destiny, only to find out that it was not! But Saul's response was priceless! He made a decision to destroy his blueprint of success instantly, which was the persecution of Christians, and asked Jesus, saying, "What would you have me do?" Saul embraced God's blueprints for his life without getting all of the details or information. He willingly humbled himself and obeyed the voice of God. As great as this sounds, it can also be scary what Saul did.

In many ways, Paul made a decision on the spot to start over again. Can you imagine spending your entire life thinking that you were supposed to be heading in one direction but come to find out that God has a different path for you to follow? I remember when I had to accept the reality that my childhood dream of becoming a medical doctor had to bow to the divine purpose of God for my life. I was convinced that I was supposed to be a medical doctor who would do ministry ad hoc when convenient. But while I was still a student in college, God began to blow up my little childhood plans! I was a student at Cornell University and had finished a tough conversation with a trusted advisor and a long-standing staff member at the school. I made the decision to switch my major from Biology/Pre-medicine to Africana Studies and Research (Africana Studies is an interdisciplinary field that studies people of African descent around the world, primarily in the United States, Africa, and the Caribbean). It was like something died inside of me. I literally had to grieve the death of my self-developed purpose and turn the car of life around to head in the direction God had revealed to me. I share this because starting over to follow God's purpose is not easy. I had to start completely over. Scooping down to pick up these pieces in my life was beyond difficult but it was necessary in order to fulfill my ultimate God-given destiny. This divine purpose was revealed to me through a series of vivid dreams that would say the same thing: I have called you to preach, teach, and counsel! "No! No! No!" was my constant response. This is not what I spent over twenty years preparing myself for. I was matriculating through this prestigious Ivy League university with aspirations of becoming a brain surgeon. I did not leave Atlanta to become a professional minister or a teacher and surely not a counselor.

Yet, God's hand on my life was so irresistible, and my sincere desire to please God shifted my entire life. As I stated earlier, I changed my major and started a new trajectory towards God's purpose and no longer my own. But I knew that it was the thing to do! I wanted God's blueprint for my life and not my own. I knew inside that true success, prosperity, and contentment would only come from living the life that I was predestined to live. Honestly, my journey since that point has been filled with many unexpected surprises, difficult challenges, tons of missteps, and several battle scars. I have had to rebuild my life 3-4 times within a span of a few years. The journey to fulfill God's purpose and not mine has not been an easy one, but it has all been worth it! I have discovered that every experience you have in life is designed to prepare you for each aspect of your life's purpose and destiny. Life is indeed the greatest classroom for destiny, and the Holy Spirit is the best teacher! Although my life has not unfolded in the ways I dreamed and thought it would, I can declare with full faith and confidence that I am in the center of God's will for my life. I am living on purpose and in purpose. Only God has those plans, and I want to share them with you. Are you open to them? Are you open even if it means having to start over again?

Starting Over Again

One of the most challenging things to do in life is to start over. But I want to encourage you not to view starting over as a bad thing per se. I know that it is hard to see something to which you have given your blood, sweat, tears, time, and effort fall apart or come to an abrupt end, right in front of your eyes. But perhaps, God is giving you an opportunity to do something different. The truth of the matter is, sometimes what you had and what you thought was so great really was a hindrance to you moving into the greater picture of what God has for your life. Sometimes, in order to be prepared for what is ahead of you, God will allow your next step up to be down. But the step down is not to harm you or to hurt you or to take from you; instead, it is to prune you and refine you so that when God takes you up to the next place, you can truly handle and maintain what He has for you.

However, most people when they have a fresh start, go right back to their past behaviors, practices, people, places, and mindsets. When you do this, you are simply replicating what you just left. Why would you lose everything, choose to take a step down, then be elevated back up and then recreate what God tried to pull you from in the first place? A part of the reason why some people do this is because even though where you left was not what God had for you, it was comfortable, familiar and you knew how to handle that.

But for people who know that God has more for them, they must also be willing to jump out into the deep and embrace something new. Get the hunger to pursue the unfamiliar. I challenge you today to reject the familiar and to embrace something completely different. This is your season to go to new places, meet new people, try new things, expand your thinking, broaden your experiences, get out of the comfort zone of your life, and allow God to enrich you and expand you because you are far greater than you could ever imagine or think.

The Divine Roadmap

Once you know your purpose and have a vision from God that has restrained you from going your own way, now you have to create a roadmap to guide you on your journey. Just like a natural road trip, you need to know your destination, the route you are taking, the method of transportation you are going to use, and the people who will be going on this trip with you. Here are some practical steps to take.

Write It Down

First, you must write down clear vision and mission statements. Writing down clear vision and mission statements is determining the route and destination of your destiny journey. Habakkuk 2:2 NKJV says, *"Then the LORD answered me and said: Write the vision and make it plain upon tablets, that he may run who reads it."* Vision is so important that you must clearly write it down because it provides the goals and aspirations of something to come in the future. It is not yet in your now or reality, but because God has given you this vision, you begin to clearly state it in your present as if it is already yours. Habakkuk 2:3 NLT clearly supports this by saying, *"This vision is for a future time. It describes the end, and it will be fulfilled. If it seems slow in coming, wait patiently, for it will surely take place. It will not be delayed."* Live in the now as if the future is your present reality. This is essential to setting the proper pace to fully materializing your vision in life. But in order to have a clear vision, you must also write a concise mission statement. The mission is slightly different from the vision statement in that it provides the overall purpose and primary objectives. It is what you plan to do in your now to reach your vision. It sets the framework for why you exist. You write it down because it makes it official for you. It demonstrates to God and to yourself that you value the vision and mission God gave you by being a faithful steward of the information. Further, as good as your memory may be (or not), it is important to write out your vision and mission statements so that you do not forget this vital information. Losing sight of your purpose can happen not only due to physical memory loss but primarily through disappointments and setbacks. Obstacles in life have a real way of causing you to abandon your original vision and mission or question if this is the correct one in the first place. However, having your mission and vision statements written down in a visible and safe place allows you to revisit it in the difficult seasons of life, so you can gain strength and redirection for your journey to destiny. In reality, once you start your journey to destiny, you will have some serious experiences that can shake you at your core. But having succinct vision and mission statements may be the only thing you have to hold onto until you see what will happen in the future.

There are two other important reasons for writing your vision and mission statements, though they have nothing to do with you directly. One, a part of the prophetic instructions to Habakkuk in writing the vision on tablets was to allow those who read it to run or move quickly towards that end goal. So writing down your vision and mission helps those whom God has assigned to help you facilitate the speedy movement of your purpose in the same direction you are heading to. Anyone with purpose knows that he or she cannot accomplish it by himself or herself. You need partnership and support from those who believe in you and are willing to lend their knowledge, experience, resources, and connections to help you. With that said, showing your team clearly written vision and mission statements will make your purpose manifest smoother and quicker than expected. If things are not moving as fast as they could, it may be that you do not have clearly written vision and mission statements. You may be saying that you do have your vision and mission statements written down and have showed the documentation to those that work with you. Well beloved, just because it is written down does not mean that it is from God or that it is clear.

The second reason is that writing your mission and vision statements makes you accountable to the people who are aware of your statements. When there are people who see your mission and vision statements and buy into the idea, it is important to deliver what you promised. Now, let me be direct and say that things happen in life to make us want to run in the opposite direction of what we have written down. That is quite natural; however, our word is important in terms of achieving success, especially if you said, "God said!" Do not run away from or be surprised by the demand to stay true to your vision and mission from those who believe in you. This is a part of authentic leadership and a vital part of finding success in your purpose: leaders take full responsibility for either upholding or abandoning their written vision and mission.

Method of Transportation

The second tool to putting your road trip together for your journey is to decide your method of transportation. If you were going to rent a vehicle, you have several options: sedan, SUV, minivan, full passenger van, luxury, or convertible. Once you decide on the style of car you desire to take, you have to determine the size of the vehicle be it compact, economy, midsize or full. Then it gets even more specific, down to the make and model of the vehicle. I say all of this because being specific about transportation is important to making sure your trip is successful and smooth. You cannot use a vehicle that is too small or outside of your budget and expect to have an enjoyable or effective journey. Your method of transportation in the journey of destiny is found in identifying your natural and spiritual gifts that are directly connected to fulfilling your purpose. We discussed natural and spiritual gifts earlier, and I hope you are clear about what they are. Otherwise, you will face constant challenges on this trip. Nonetheless, if you are reading this, I am confident that you are aware of that. With that said, you must be clear about the specific gifts that are needed on each leg of the journey. Your gifts shift and adjust based upon your environment and the issues you need to address in a given situation. For instance, let us say that your vision and mission statements center around the use of communication to motivate people. Well, communication is both verbal and non-verbal. You may start your journey in the vehicle of speaking but hit a detour on the trip, which presents a situation that requires more written communication rather than verbal. Your ability to shift gears will help you continue to progress and thrive in the face of challenges. In this example, for instance, your speaking gifts may have to take a backseat while your written skills sit upfront.

Riding Partners

Nothing makes a road trip more exciting than having the right people on the trip with you. You may find that some of the people who start off riding with you may get out at different stops on the trip. Further, the person who was in the front with you may end up switching with someone who started on the backseat. Be flexible and sensitive to the dynamics associated with people switching in, moving around, or leaving the vehicle of your life all together. But allow me to take this discussion of riding partners beyond people to your gifts themselves. Now, I want you to see your gifts and skills as both the vehicle and riding partners in your journey. One of the ways to get the fullest use of your gifts is to make decisions that bring your natural and spiritual gifts closer together. Do not be afraid of being ambidextrous with your gifts. This means you are able to use both your natural and spiritual gifts equally as well. Let me put it another way: engage in both your Kingdom and Marketplace purposes. Many Kingdom people tend to seek God for clarity on what they should be doing in their religious institution, in terms of purpose, but they often separate that from what they should be doing in their cultural mountain. I am saying that moving your vehicle in a direction and on a route that makes your Kingdom and Marketplace assignments closely connected will produce great returns and dividends in your life. See both callings as equal riding partners in the vehicle of life.

When I made the decision to become a professional minister, I focused on the Kingdom assignment aspect of it; however, as I progressed in life, I realized that I had a Marketplace side to my purpose. Life brought me to the door of Law Enforcement. Until this point, I had not seriously considered a career in this field and thought it would be dissonant with my ministerial purpose. Was I ever so wrong in this thought! Law enforcement has strongly informed my ministry and vice versa. I know that being a minister makes me an excellent officer, and being an officer makes me a dynamic minister. When I first entered the noble profession of Law Enforcement, I would go back and visit my purpose statement from college, which was "to preach, to teach, and to counsel," and I recognized that this field allowed me to be a teacher and counselor of sorts. So I could move in that direction with more peace of mind. And, an amazing thing happened to me as to bringing my Kingdom and Marketplace assignments closer together: I found myself fulfilling more aspects of my overall vision and mission statements inside of my Marketplace assignment than I did outside of it, and the same applied to my Kingdom calling.

For example, I worked in the non-profit sector and government as an administrator. I also had a brief stint in education as a substitute teacher. But I found that as I tried to find employment in these fields again later in life, things were not happening. My mother told me one day as I started my journey in Law Enforcement that the doors that had been shut would open up inside Policing. I scratched my head because I did not readily see how I could be an educator, administrator, and community advocate inside Law Enforcement. However, today, I can attest that I am all of the above while still serving as a Police Officer. I have found such fulfillment in this aspect of my Marketplace assignment. But in order to have found this fulfillment, I had to be willing to take both hands off my Kingdom assignment as a ministerial leader and place one of them in the Marketplace through a government job. I encourage you to resist the urge to separate what you do at church from what you do at work during the week. I insist that you see your work for God as a co-partner with what you do for your organization or your own business.

Break the Route Up

The last tool in putting together your road map of purpose is to get a large picture of your journey and then break it up into smaller segments. I have taken some long road trips especially when I was in college. I have driven from Upstate New York and New York City to Georgia a few times before. The one thing that helped me survive this over 15 hours road trip was to break it up in my head into segments. I would say to myself, "OK, once I reach Interstate 40 from Interstate 81 in Tennessee, then I know I was these certain hours away from Atlanta." This made the trip less overwhelming because I could digest 4 hours much easier than 15. On the journey of life, it is important to build your life in phases by strategically developing your overall plan into a step-by-step approach. The adage "Rome was not built in a day" certainly applies to this concept. It takes time, effort, and energy to reach your goal but you must be intentional and consistent. I hear the words of my spiritual father ringing in my ears from when I was a newly minted Pastoral resident fresh out of seminary: You have to build your life in phases or otherwise you will get frustrated and make dangerous missteps. We see this same principle working in the life of major leaders in the Scriptures. For instance, in the story of Joseph as recorded in Genesis 37, he had two dreams about his future as a leader, yet the manifestation of that dream was unfolded in phases not in one lump sum. It took him being thrown into the pit, sold to Potiphar, placed in jail through false allegations, and then being summoned to the palace to eventually serve as Prime Minister before he could get himself to the full realization of his vision. That is why he could declare with confidence to his brothers in Genesis 50:19-20 NKJV that states, *"Joseph said to them, 'Do not be afraid, for am I in the place of God? But as for you, you meant evil against me; but God meant it for good, in order to bring it about as it is this day, to save many people alive.'"* Another great example of this is King David.

Although he was anointed to be King by Samuel in 1 Samuel 16:13, it took many years of running from the current leader, King Saul, many disappointments, and several battles before he experienced the manifestation of his appointment. David had to build his life in segments along his journey. But each leg of the trip was purposeful and necessary to develop and prepare him for His reign as King of the joint kingdoms of Israel and Judah. Take a step back from trying to accomplish the whole picture and focus on each part step by step. You may be pleasantly surprised at how much more you accomplish and how fast you will move towards your destiny.

Purpose Keeps You Moving

Knowing and believing in your purpose will give you the discipline required to follow the direction set before you step by step, despite the seeming obstacles and setbacks that may arise. I remember when I was going through the interview process to become a senior pastor at a church a few years back. Some of the members of the search committee told me I was the frontrunner candidate. However, once the vote was taken, I was not the first choice but the second. The final decision not to select me as the lead pastor was devastating to me because I sincerely believed this was where I was supposed to be at that time in my life. Nonetheless, I was clear and confident about my purpose. This purpose gave me direction around this roadblock in my journey. In addition to my personal assurance of purpose was the great support of wise counsel I received from some trusted people.

As we shift from Principle 1, I want to highlight the importance of having people who can remind you of your purpose and affirm your direction in the face of disappointments. In this particular instance about the ministry, it was my mother's prophetic declarations and surprise visit from one of my Ghanaian brothers who came to Atlanta to walk the grounds of the church for prayer that kept me focused. My mother's counsel and decrees reminded me of King Lemuel's mother's counsel to him, as found in the later part of Proverbs. The value of counsel from wise people, most especially parents and seasoned people, is absolutely essential to purpose and direction. They have travelled many of the same roads you will traverse in life. Their wisdom and experience can prevent you from some falls and unnecessary detours if you will listen and believe. Even Samson in his self-willed independence from his Nazarene vows (as recorded in the book of Judges) knew the value of consulting one's parents. When my Pastor friend from Ghana came to Atlanta, he walked with me on the property and prayed a simple prayer: if it is the will of God for David to be here AND to prosper in this place, then release the ministry by opening the doors to him. If it is not the will of God for David to be here AND to prosper in this place, then do not release it. Keep the door closed! That prayer taught me that it takes more than a desire to be in a place, it takes the desire to know God's will and to be where that will of God will prosper in your hands. Well, God opened the door and allowed me to serve that congregation; and as God would have it, the membership increased rapidly, and the spiritual commitment of the members soared beautifully. Take heart, beloved, in knowing that recognizing and embracing God's purpose for your life will position you on the path that will get you there as long as you are going with a set of directions to help you make it there safely. Trust God and keep moving by faith and vision.

[35]

PRINCIPLE 2

Discovering and Prioritizing Your Gift Increases Your Value

Prioritizing Your Gifts

In Principle 1, we discussed that you have both natural and spiritual gifts inside of you. In Principle 2, I want to drill down into this a little more. The discovery of your gifts is vital to the successful realization of your purpose because it gives direction to your life and it helps you to recognize what brings results—that is, what works and what does not work. Is that not what success is really about at its core? Knowing by experience, pattern and principle what works, why it works, where it works, when it works, and with whom it works. The "what" here is your gifts, talents, and abilities. Then from there, you can take that data, reproduce it at will, and get the same results if not better. Discovery is the first step in the journey to really working your room! I will discuss the concept of "working your room" later in the book but for now, let me say that working your room is about maximizing your moment when you gain access to it, with the determination to be successful. Dr. Paula A. Price, a leading apostolic voice in our time, states that one of the marks of the apostolic mantle is that God reinforces you because He knows that you will always bring Him a win! If God knows that wherever He places you in the world, you will have the determination and drive to be prosperous and overly successful, then He will constantly back you up with the resources of Heaven to ensure your repeated victory. A key factor in having this unrelenting drive is knowing, without doubt and with confidence, what your gifts are! While the discovery of your gifts through a prophetic declaration, natural observations, and/or an assessment is the first step, it is not the only one.

Once you have found out what your natural and spiritual gifts are, then you must take the next step, and that is prioritizing your gifts. Prioritizing your gifts means that while you may have many wonderful abilities, you have to place them on a rank or scale of importance and usefulness based upon the task and situation at hand. One thing God revealed to me years ago is that End Time people, especially youth and young adults, would have multiple gifts inside of them and at work through their lives. This is a great reality and is much needed for the Kingdom and the Marketplace. However, this can be an impediment if the gifts are not prioritized. My mother recognized that I had many natural and spiritual gifts inside of me at a young age. However, she told me something very interesting. She said, "Son, your problem is not that you do not have gifts but that you have a lot of them! Therefore, if you are not careful, you can become the 'jack of all trades but the master of none.'" Again, it is great that you have many gifts, passions, and interests. You may be as I am, with the ability to put your hands in many different "pots," so to speak, and still get great results. This is excellent, beloved. However, to gain ground in your life and to establish stability, you must get a clear handle on the more pronounced or dominant gifts in you and those that will serve in a complementary or supportive role.

Matching Gift with Purpose

One of the ways to come to this determination is to return to your mission and purpose statement and ask yourself, "Which gift is the best one to bring this mission and purpose to pass, with the highest degree of excellence, ease, and integrity?" You have to decide which of the gifts will be the foundation to your image and brand. Yes, you may have ten excellent natural and spiritual gifts that make up the total sum of you; but I want to lovingly and gently push you to pick the leading or dominant one! I know this may be a little challenging, even nerve wrecking. People typically do not like to narrow down their options to just one thing and figure out how that one thing connects to all the other things in the mix called YOU. But it is absolutely essential to experiencing success in your purpose because your ability to prioritize your gifts with a clear sense of what is the lead or dominant gift will automatically increase your value in the Marketplace and the Kingdom alike. Ask yourself today, "What gift in my storehouse of abilities positions me to be of most value to the audience or cultural mountain I am assigned to?" Furthermore, you have to press in to your inner self and ask, "Is this gift still in demand as I originally presented it or does it need a facelift, makeover or a total renovation?" These deep but necessary questions will help point serious purpose seekers towards the needed process of picking one ability that will take the lead. Then it progresses you towards the specific and intentional development of that ability. Ultimately, you will strategically design a system and mechanism with your dominant gift as the heart that pumps, funnels, and supplies your purpose with all of your other gifts. From here, you can branch off like arteries and veins through the body of your destiny to produce several streams of possibilities, ventures, enterprises, and businesses. But they all flow in and out of the heart of who makes you unique and distinct. Arriving and surviving in this place, this reality is what makes you of great value to the world.

Companies, organizations, tribes, affinity groups, and people in general are looking for leaders who have their fingers firmly (but not glued to the point that you cannot adjust) pressed to the pulse of what makes them exist and thrive. So it is not about just knowing your purpose and your gifts in order to achieve success and fulfillment. Rather, you have to understand what is the most valuable gift people are looking for and are willing to invest in. For instance, you may be an excellent baker of deserts. Your personal favorite is making and designing cakes of all flavors. You are good at baking cakes and people like them. However, people tend to purchase and rave about your gingerbread cookies. You like baking gingerbread cookies but it is not what you consider as your lead baking gifting. Allow me to say something frankly but with all love intended. Another factor in prioritizing gifts for the result of increased value is to move beyond how you feel about your gifts to accepting the gift that brings consistent results! Just because you personally like making cakes because it reminds of you a loved one who taught you to bake, does not mean that people want to buy your cakes. But they DO want to buy your gingerbread cookies! So do you put cakes in the front of gingerbread cookies because of your feelings or do you push your feelings aside and focus on what is working? Success requires us to put our feelings and emotions in their proper place and out of the way of doing what is best for our overall destiny.

Three Questions for Prioritizing Gifts

I have indirectly given some steps to prioritizing your gifts towards determining your dominant gift. Allow me to state them more directly. There are at least three questions that you can ask yourself to help you figure out how to place your abilities in order of importance and dominance. The first question is, "What gift (natural or spiritual) constantly produces positive results in my set place?" The heart of this question pushes you towards recognizing patterns of success based upon public responses to your gift in your sphere of purpose (i.e. career, cultural mountain, or venture). You cannot truly experience consistent victory if you cannot pinpoint what brings you success. This gift may not be your favorite one or the one that seems like the easiest one to bring result. However, it should be a gift that comes forth from you with ease, and appears to everyone else that you could work with it, even if you were blindfolded and with your hands tied behind your back. That is the key here. You may have your own internal and private wrestling with your gifts and your progress. But when you get in front of people or begin to do your "thing," it looks so easy and awesome to them. As a result, people, organizations, and enterprises gravitate towards you and want you to offer your goods to them and as well consolidate their efforts.

The second question you should ask yourself to help you prioritize your gifts is, "Which of my gifts make me unique from other people in the same field or work?" I love this scripture in 1 Corinthians 12:4-7 AMP because it lays a solid foundation for this question as Paul writes to a church full of gifted people with questions about how all these gifts work together in unity:

> Now there are [distinctive] varieties of spiritual gifts [special abilities given by the grace and extraordinary power of the Holy Spirit operating in believers], but it is the same Spirit [who grants them and empowers

believers]. And there are [distinctive] varieties of ministries and service, but it is the same Lord [who is served]. And there are [distinctive] ways of working [to accomplish things], but it is the same God who produces all things in all believers [inspiring, energizing, and empowering them]. But to each one is given the manifestation of the Spirit [the spiritual illumination and the enabling of the Holy Spirit] for the common good.

The truth about gifts is that thousands of people may have the same gift as you have, but there is no one who can operate in your gift like you! Let us say you have the gift of logistics. You are good at what has to do with managing, planning, implementing, and overseeing the smooth, two-way movement of products between entities. Well, thousands of others are also good at logistics. So now, you have to clearly identify and succinctly state to people what makes your logistics gift unique in comparison to others with similar ability. This is challenging for some Kingdom people to do because we are not often encouraged to brag and boast about why we are outstanding and better than the rest. The Kingdom teaches us to remain humble and to be unassuming. While this is true to a certain extent, it has to be tempered and balanced with the understanding that we are called to shine for God in the world. We house within our earthen vessel a great treasure as Paul the Apostle tells us in 2 Corinthians 4:7. This treasure consists of our gifts and abilities birthed and bathed in the brilliant light of God's presence in us. So we demonstrate, discuss, and showcase these gifts not to brag about ourselves per se but to point people to the awesomeness of our God working through us. Philippians 2:13 says, *"For it is God who works in you both to will and to do for His good pleasure."* Therefore, we must have a humble confidence when it comes to our gifts! In fact, meekness is not weakness but it is the ability to know, own, and live in and up to your purpose, gift, and power, though you have to control it to the place that it does not overpower or puff you up, lest you to wreck your own progress. Do not be afraid any longer to confidently and clearly declare to people what your primary gift is and how it is distinct from the rest.

From here, we can fully launch into the last question, "What gift causes people of influence to consider me and my contributions' value?" When you can identify what that gift is and can clearly articulate what makes your gift unique, people of influence and means will pay attention to you. They will open doors and grant opportunities that will give you exposure, resources, and experience at the next level. We will discuss this more in Section III. I made a decision a few years back that I wanted to live a life where purpose, compensation, and impact intersected! This is one of my guiding mantras in life and it governs the types of decisions I make, the opportunities I accept (and do not accept), and the circle of people I surround myself with. This question also makes you uncomfortable as to entertaining people, places, and things that want you to use your gift for their benefit but do not demonstrate that they value you and your gift. Let me put it another way. When you identify that your primary gift is valuable, then you will refuse to let people use and abuse you! But you have to believe within yourself that what you have to offer is of high value.

Now, let me state this clearly. You cannot advertise something that you cannot deliver! That is like buying one brand of soft drink that promises to refresh your dry mouth, only to drink it and find out your mouth is left in a worse condition than before. No! Refrain from overselling and under-delivering. People over promise and oversell their gifts often because they do not think that what they have is good enough. I want to encourage you to believe that you are good enough. We all need to make improvements and continue to develop ourselves. But if you do not embrace and love who you are and what you offer at its base level, then any additions, improvements, and advancements will be faulty because the foundation—your mental approval and acceptance of your identity—is corrupt. Your foundation is riddled with self-hatred, low self-esteem, the despising of your humble or small beginnings, the shame of your past, the avoidance of your flaws and issues…the list goes on and on. Anyone who knows about the foundations of buildings knows that foundations cannot have holes in them even at the microscopic level because if moisture or other substances get in through the openings, it will corrupt the foundation. If your house is built on a sandy foundation, then your house will not endure the storms that life will bring. This is what Jesus was talking about in the Parable of the builder in Matthew 7:24-27. Build on a solid foundation and people will value you. If your foundation is weak and non-sturdy, then you will find yourself constantly in the company of people who are of lesser knowledge, possession, and influence than you are, and such people will use your greater knowledge, possession, and influence for their benefit while convincing you that you are nothing and need them. This is the doorway to abuse and belittlement. Open your eyes and see that God has placed something of tremendous worth inside of you, which the world needs to see and experience. Avoid people who cannot value you through their words, actions, and deeds but want to constantly use—abuse—you. But this all starts with YOU making a decision to pinpoint and stick with the gift that will make people treat you with respect and value, and that brings financial stability and contentment to your life.

Determining Value

While we are discussing identifying your top gift that people count valuable, we must understand and recognize that value shifts based upon trends and occurrences in the society and the marketplace. Therefore, in order to maintain our demand and need in the Marketplace and the Kingdom, you must always be willing to redefine and reinvent yourself to stay current and firmly planted with the movement. This is a major challenge for many people because in general, people do not like change. We fight and resist change. But, the only constant thing in life is CHANGE! Change is inevitable and necessary; and those who are committed to maintaining value and achieving success in their purpose must be willing to change as needed without compromising their integrity, purpose, and core values. The inverse is also true. When you have a clear purpose that is rooted in Kingdom ethics and surrounded by core values, you will not devalue yourself just to make money, get a position, or mount a platform. This is where some Kingdom people are missing the mark. You are willing to do ANYTHING to be successful. Beloved, when you are a person who has identified his or her gift and placed value on it, then you do not have to compromise and corrupt your name, reputation, and virtues in order to move up the ladder of life. This is why you have to be careful not to only measure your value in terms of money or influence. Yes, it is true that most people define their value by how much money they have or the amount of material goods they have amassed. But when you know your gifts and why you have them, you will find that your value is not in money but in your gifts. Knowing how to effectively use your gifts in the market or industry it is designed to shine, will increase your value every time. May I submit to you that you have three sets of gifts that are of more value than money, though they will lead you to earning more money and will open doors for you when you do not have money. I like to call them the Three "S" Equities.

The Three "S" Equities

I have the privilege of listening to people's journey and stories on a daily basis. One thing I have noticed when people are sharing tales about their passion or destiny is that finances and the lack of resources are one of the main things that stand between them and their goal. Yes, we need money or equity without any question. Nevertheless, I want to show you that you already have three other types of equities that, when used together, can be more powerful than financial equity.

Sweat. This means that you use the gifts, skills, and efforts you already have to get started on your dream. Sweat equity requires you to work hard, loose sleep, adjust your schedule, and transfer your fun or leisure time towards the work required to get your ideas off the ground. You will only get out of it what you put in. Sweat equity demands more creativity from you because you have to search out free resources to help you get started and you have to find ways to make a "dollar out of fifteen cents!" The bottom line is that if you want your dream to become a reality, you have to get busy working where you are and with what you have, rather than sit around waiting for a million dollars to fall out of the sky into your lap.

[45]

Social. This refers to the relationships you have with people and organizations. If you have developed and maintained genuine and authentic relationships with others, then they will help you without any reservation. They will lend you their information, connections, finances, and time to help your dream become a reality. The challenge for most people is that they have, for example, 2,000 Facebook "friends" but no REAL friends in their lives. We do not value and cultivate relationships anymore. Keeping your friendships intact requires WORK! You have to communicate on a regular basis not just when you need something or have an emergency! And you have to be available to support their dreams and visions as well.

Spiritual. As a covenant person, you have been given great resources from Heaven to help you advance into your purpose in life. One of these resources is FAVOR! Favor is God breaking the rules on your behalf and granting access to things that you normally would not be able to obtain. Favor overlooks your shortcomings, mishaps, frailties, and inabilities and causes you to overcome every obstacle, barrier, and hindrance along the way. If you really understood that ALL of the resources of HEAVEN are backing you up, then you would get busy TODAY working on your dream. The real issue is that we allow fear, procrastination, insecurities, people's opinions, and, for some, the fear of hard, consistent work, keep us from moving closer to our goal. For many, saying that you do not have the money and the time to reach your dream is a cover-up for the real issue: YOU ARE HOLDING YOURSELF BACK. Today, I pray that the God of all grace will give you the courage and drive to use the three equities He has given you, thus causing you to prosper beyond your imagination. May the three equities bring you into the fourth one, which is FINANCIAL equity, thereby causing your reach and influence to extend to the ends of the earth in the name of our Lord Jesus Christ.

PRINCIPLE 3

Determining the Value of Your Gift Directly Affects Your Demand Level

This is a good place to dig deeper into the theme scripture for this book, Proverbs 18:16, *"A man's gift makes room for him, and brings him before great men."* The theologian in me must explain this scripture so that it can be applied appropriately to our discussion on gifts. The word "gift" in Proverbs 18:16 in the original language is "mattan." It means gifts, offerings, or presents. This is important to point out because we have been discussing gifts in terms of natural and spiritual abilities. But in the text, the term gift is actually connected to giving monetary gifts or presents to a person in hopes of winning them over and gaining favor with the individual. This notion is supported in a few other places in the Old Testament, where the same word "mattan" is used. For example, Genesis 34:12 talks about the dowry paid to gain a young lady for a wife. We also see this in two other places, Proverbs: 19:6 (many will entreat the favour of the prince: and every man is a friend to him that giveth gifts) and 21:14 (a gift in secret pacifieth anger: and a reward in the bosom strong wrath).

The Value in Gifts

Giving gifts has a double-fold importance for people who are living on purpose. One, when you give gifts to people, you are demonstrating your understanding of the value of being in their space. According to our focal scripture, giving the right kind of gift will create a space for you in front of important people. Let me put it another way: you cannot get the support of important people, movers, and shakers, if you do not add value to their space. If you want to progress in your purpose, you must recognize that you need to have something of value and worth that others also consider valuable and useful. However, our culture has become plagued with an entitlement mentality. People feel that people owe them something or that they should automatically get opportunities. In some instances, this has merit but in most, it does not. If you think that you are entitled to be in the company or to have audience with influential people who can help you move further in life, then you either will not keep their attention long enough to make an impression or you will be escorted out of their presence just as quickly as you entered. Entitlement gives off a distasteful energy and feeling to people of substance. One of the reasons this happens is that most people of value have worked diligently and endlessly to accomplish their goals in life, along with the assistance of people who believed in them and invested in their future. They know first-hand that entitlement did not get them to where they are in life now. There are certain people in my life right now that I hold in high regard because of the role they have played in assisting me in moving closer to my goals in life. I recognize who they are and I value their time, expertise, and space to the point that I rarely come empty-handed in my visits to their space. What I mean by this is that I bring either a physical gift or my spiritual and natural gifts to the encounter to demonstrate my appreciation.

Dummy Mission

We see this concept in the Old Testament. For instance, when Saul, before he was appointed king over Israel, was sent on a journey to search his father's missing donkeys, he could not find them anywhere. I love this story because the trip, in God's plan, was never about the donkeys but about the discovery of purpose. I like to call Saul's trip a "dummy mission." When I say dummy, I am not saying that to mean ignorant, but rather to mean a fake covering the real. This trip for Saul was really a mission to usher him into becoming king.

As Saul and his servants searched for days for the donkeys with no success, the servant suggested in 1 Samuel 9 that they find the seer—prophets were called seers before they were called prophets. They found a lady and asked if she had seen Samuel, the seer of the time. She told them that the man of God had gone ahead of them, and on hearing that, his servant asked, "What are we going to give him?" The servant realized that one did not go to the prophet empty-handed because he was considered valuable. His information is valuable! His words and time were of top value and premium. I want to encourage you to consider the fact that recognizing the value of your gifts as well as acknowledging the value of other people will place you in constant demand!

People will send for you all the time with a constant request for your gifts and talents. While you may not bring cash or expensive presents, your spiritual and natural abilities will function like currency in the world. So beloved, make a decision today to become more intimately acquainted with your gifts and determine its value. Then make the bold and courageous move to present it to the world. You will be amazed at how many people will also recognize the value of your gift and then create a space for you to come where they are. But if you do not know the value of your gifts, then you can never expect to be in a company of great people.

The Danger of Not Knowing Your Value

I am an avid observer of people's behaviors and a listener of their narratives. It amazes me how many people have great gifts that are actually working for them but do not know or own the value of their gifts. This is one of the most dangerous things for a person of purpose: not to recognize your value. Furthermore, it becomes even more problematic if your enemies and competitors recognize your value before you do because you will become an object of abuse. People will use you up and then throw you away when they are done with you or when you wake up and come to your senses. Do you want to know why some people keep being used? Do you know why certain people abuse you over and over? Perhaps it is because while you may know your gifts, you allow past experiences, low self-worth, and obstacles cause you to overlook or underrate your value. This under-valuing hits the nostrils of haters like fear to the senses of dogs. They smell it from a mile away. They pick up on the fact that you do not fully know or embrace your value. Therefore, they will pretend to invite you to the table of opportunity, where they want you to present your gift, but it is designed to use and drain you. And because you have not determined to stand by your value, you will take any door that opens to you without discerning if the door is sincerely for you or it is designed to hurt you. You have to know when to say "NO!" Not every door is for you. Not every smiling face values the greatness inside of you. There are times you need to take your knowledge, experience, and abilities, leave the table, and exit the room without looking back.

Yes, there are some legitimate reasons for walking away from something like domestic abuse in relationships or unethical practices in a business/organization. Some people feel like they have something to prove by staying in a toxic environment or relationship. Like in some twisted way, you are demonstrating your value. Not so! You have to know when to stay and when to go. As my older deacons say, "You have to know when to hold them and know when to fold them." What I am talking about is when you know that you are an asset to a person/place/thing, but that person/place/thing takes you for granted and mishandles you. They steal your ideas and present them as their own creation OR they tell you that you are not as gifted or talented as you think you are; even though, you are the one—the in-house expert—making everything in their company function. Maybe someone—your date—makes you feel unattractive and undesirable but gets mad because you get so much attention from people when you are out in public. These are all classic signs that you are connected to a person/place/thing that recognizes that you bring great worth to them but want to convince you otherwise so they can CONTROL and MONOPOLIZE what you bring.

If you leave, then they know they would go down in production, function, and presentation. God wants you to make a deep resolution today that you will not allow people to take advantage of your gifts because you know your value! I stand in agreement with you today by faith and declare that the experience of having people take advantage of your gifts is over TODAY! With that said, however, I want to submit to you that sometimes, abuse and rejection can be the best 'gift' you have ever received in terms of determining your value, especially when you are blinded by the need to prove people wrong, even though they will never change their perspective of you.

Necessity of Rejection

When we experience rejection in life, especially from those we least expected it from, it can leave deep wounds that seem like they will remain open forever. However, when you look back and reflect on the journey that rejection took you on, you may come to the realization that although it was painful, it was QUITE NECESSARY. If it were not for the rejection, then you would not be who you are today, doing what you are doing and moving into your destiny. The rejection that you experienced was designed to reposition you from a place of stagnation, complacency, and mediocrity into a space of progression, ambition, and excellence. Turn your tears into laughter and your mourning into dancing. Rejection actually did you a huge favor: it gave you the swift kick into gear that you needed to move yourself forward so that you would not miss your moment with destiny.

A great biblical story about the helpfulness of rejection is found in Judges 11 about a man named Jephthah. He is described as a mighty man of valor, which means he is skilled and successful at winning wars. This was his gift, and he knew his value. However, he was the son of a harlot and lived in the house of his father and half-brothers. In the course of time, his half-brothers kicked him out of the house and told him that he would never have an inheritance in their father's house. So Jephthah left and went to the land of Tob. The rejection that he experienced in his father's house was essential to his purpose in life because it literally repositioned him for destiny. Repositioned here means to place in a different position. It also means to change the image of something, to target a new or wider coverage or market. God will use rejection to push us out of a place that we refuse to move ourselves. If I use my biblical imagination, I can imagine Jephthah trying to convince his brothers that he was worthy of being accepted by them despite his condition of being born illegitimately. We cannot waste precious time trying to live down our past. We all have made mistakes—some private and some public. So do not allow people to hold you hostage to those things and cause you to lower your opinion of yourself. This will negatively affect your self-worth and your progression. You will be amazed at how many people specialize in making others feel worthless because of their past mistakes. The funny thing about it is that the person, who is pointing the finger at you often, has more issues than you have. Yes, criticism is important for growth and development but you can only trust it if the person who is giving it has your best interest at heart.

Another thing I can visualize Jephthah doing in Gilead was trying to make himself fit in with his brothers and the inhabitants of Gilead. Sometimes, we do the same thing! We try to make ourselves fit into places that we were never designed to fit into. It is like forcing a square peg to fit into a round hole. The reality is that if people do not recognize and acknowledge your value on their own, then there is very little you can do to change their minds without devaluing and demeaning yourself. When you shift your focus away from developing your gifts to convincing people to change their perspective of you, then you also stop engaging in the things that make you valuable. When you decrease in value, you also begin to decrease in demand! So God does us a favor by allowing people, places, and things to reject us and as a result pushes us out of a place we clamor to hold onto.

You know that it is God who pushes you out because the place you are pushed into is a good place. When Jephthah left Gilead, he went to the land of Tob. Tob in the original language means a "good place." While in Tob, Jephthah was able to reengage with his gift and increase his value. The scripture tells us that vain men came to find Jephthah in the fields, and they began to go on fighting missions. This is great because Jephthah is a mighty man of valor. His gift and strength is best seen and displayed when he is fighting and training his army in successful war tactics. As a result of his exploits in Tob, the elders of Gilead sent for Jephthah to return home to help them defeat their enemy. When Jephthah increased his value, he increased his demand! This would not have happened however, if he had not been rejected from the same place he thought he needed. The reality was they needed him more than he needed them. Divine rejection is so necessary for purpose-filled people because if you stay in a place that has demeaned you too long, then you will become your own worst enemy.

No Self Sabotage

When you have greatness inside of you but have spent significant time in environments that have harassed, belittled, and marginalized you, then you can begin to question if you are great or have anything to contribute. These experiences are very real and damaging. However, when your life repositions you from a place of denial and rejection to a place of approval and acceptance, you have to make a shift in your mentality and perception. If not, you will be in your enlarged place, but still acting as if you are caged in! You will have people and things around you that are affirming and appreciating you on what you offer BUT because you are still acting, feeling, and thinking like you are rejected, unappreciated, and oppressed, YOU CAN SABOTAGE your elevation and increase. Are you in your destiny acting like you are still in bondage? Shine a flashlight inward to your soul and take an honest assessment. Are you really ready for your destiny or was it just lip service? Have you created a permanent, negative identity from an experience that was only temporary? Please, do not pluck up your destiny with your own hands, mouth, behavior, posture, or habits because you have not brought your mind, soul, and attitude up to where you are today. Self-sabotage is a result of lack of understanding of one's value. You begin to believe and internalize the lies you have been fed. Then you start to do, say, and present things that directly destroy what you have been praying for. Self-sabotage is a dangerous practice for people of purpose. You have to address it head-on through counseling, prayer, and a support team that will hold you accountable to making healthy decisions and actions that move you towards your destiny and not away from it.

Have You Left Your Assignment too Soon?

With all of what has been stated, I must balance and present the other side of this coin. There are times that life and God will place you in environments that you are undervalued and used and you are required to stay longer than you want. If this is the case, it is designed to teach you some lessons about yourself and those using you, and to reposition yourself to gain increase. That is why it is important to properly discern the reason for every opportunity that may come your way. I could remember what happened a couple of years ago; over a few weeks, our supervisors were telling us daily during roll call not to report to the precinct before our time to leave. The reason for this instruction was that there might still be a call or case that could come up for us to address before we would leave. Coming back early meant that we would be leaving our post too soon. I must admit that getting a case when it was about the time to go home was not fun at all, but it came with the territory. It was necessary to work the full shift and not shortchange the day by leaving too soon. It is a human tendency to want to avoid that which is uncomfortable, stressful, and painful and to run towards those experiences and things that are comfortable, easy, and pleasurable. However, the reality is that if you want to really grow, progress, and produce, then you will have more of the former than the latter ones. The saying is really true: NO PAIN, NO GAIN.

When life gets stressful and overwhelming, so many people want to run away and end their assignment too soon. Some of you today as you read this can relate to this fact. You have had a job, a relationship, an idea, or an opportunity that started off great and seemed to be exactly what you were looking for. And all of a sudden, the tables turned. What started as a wonderful experience became stressful and unpleasant. Instead of sticking it out and finding ways to make it work, perhaps, you walked away and said, "I am done with this!" "I do not have to take this!"

Jacob experienced this with his father-in-law, Laban, in Genesis 30. After spending 20 years working like a slave to gain his wives and livestock, he asked to be released, to build his own life as a family man. Laban clearly states "I know from experience that I have been blessed and have increased for YOUR SAKE." Instead of releasing Jacob to do his thing, he continued to mishandle Jacob and played games to keep him imprisoned because Laban knew that if he lost Jacob, his fortunes would decrease and decline overnight. With all of this said, Jacob did something that many of us could not and would not do! So did King David when he was on the run from King

Saul. So did Hagar when she went back to stay put under the cruel management of Sarah. What am I talking about? They had the ability to stay where they were, to work out their divine strategy, and not leave because of their emotions or feelings. They stayed until GOD SAID "GO," NOT THEMSELVES SAYING "GO!" Let me be frank and say, some of you are still struggling, spinning your wheels, and misplaced because maybe—and I humbly mean maybe—you left an assignment TOO SOON; all because you were an asset and you were being mishandled, you allowed your feelings, rationalization, or other people tell you to just get up and go! I am not saying that your mistreatment was/is right (side note: I am not talking about situations of abuse and unethical/immoral practices) BUT what I am saying is that if God has put Covenant presence on your life (meaning you being there brings the blessings and favor of the LORD to that setting and all that are connected) and has placed you in a setting, then even when it is stressful, painful, and uncomfortable, there is a REASON and a PURPOSE to that! You have to endure and stay until God says, "Go!"

You will know it is time to go when (1) You have come to terms with the insecurities, flaws, and fleshly ambitions/lust that got you in a situation where you allowed a person/place/thing to convince you that you were less than what God made you to be; (2) You have a solid exit strategy that is not messy, combative, or disruptive. There is a right way to do wrong and there is a right way to leave a situation. God will give you a strategy; (3) A window/moment/opportunity will present itself to you, thus making the exit smooth and seamless; (4) Even in your leaving, the person/place/thing cannot deny that you were nothing but a blessing and increase. Even if they badmouth you for leaving and try to sabotage/blacklist you, the majority will know, without a question, that you were an asset. Then and only then can you leave and move on to your assignment with peace and with the proper backing from God to find success in your new season.

Turning Value into Demand

One of the main signs that you are experiencing success in your purpose is that your gift, ability, and talent are in demand by people and organizations who value your gift and will provide you with opportunities to utilize it with proper compensation in return. Allow me to share some steps that will help you turn the value of your gifts into something marketable and in constant demand. First, you must do research to determine the appropriate value to assign to your gift. This is crucial, as you do not want to oversell or undersell your value. Law Enforcement has taught me how to gauge the value of my time. When I work extra jobs in the city, there is a base level amount that businesses are willing to pay me just to provide police presence. You have to ask around, look online, and attend seminars where businesses and organizations are discussing what they are looking for and what they are willing to pay to get it. From there, you have to take an honest assessment to make sure that what you are offering is on par with what people are looking for. That is a part of branding yourself and your gift. A brand says that this is what you get when you buy or use this product. Therefore, the product must deliver what the brand claims it would give. Otherwise, you will lose value and as a result, you will lose demand. Once you have determined that your gift matches— and it should really surpass—what people are looking for, establish a range of value for your services and expertise. Here is an important note: because you are starting off and trying to establish yourself, be flexible and willing to negotiate your value. This is why I suggest creating a range. You have to determine how much is too low and how much is too high. There are so many people out there trying to reach their purpose just like you, so your market may be oversaturated from the jump. However, your ability to present the uniqueness of your gift in the market coupled with your flexibility will open doors for you that otherwise would stay closed.

The second thing I would suggest you do to position yourself so as to translate value into demand is to gather testimonials and data to prove your value. This is why customer service and satisfaction is so important. You want people to be so pleased with your gift that they are more than willing to share it with you and other people. Ask them to write down their opinion of your service, business, or gift. Store them in a safe place on your computer or on a hard drive so that you can retrieve it at the appropriate time. If you have a website, have a testimonial section where people can share their experience with your services. Take pictures of yourself in action, working your gift. Gather video and audio recordings of you speaking, singing, cooking, or doing whatever it is that you do. Create a portfolio that highlights your successes and accomplishments. You may need to select some people who are good at pictures and technology to capture critical moments and store it for you. This is needed because if you are trying to build a name for yourself in an industry that is oversaturated and you are unknown in, then you must have tangible proofs that you can deliver beyond your words! You have to convince the powers that be—

leaders or competitors in the industry—that you deserve an opportunity and a shot getting into the ROOM!

The third thing to creating value that places you in higher demand is administration. Having a team of people who believe in you and are willing to work alongside of you to promote your gifts is one of the factors that will either make you or break you when it comes to the dynamics of success. One of my favorite books on this topic is "The Leadership Gap" by Mr. Curtis Wallace. In his book, he suggests that the one single factor that enables one gifted leader to excel beyond another leader with equal or similar gifts is forming the right team of people to support the vision. Having a team is not enough though. You have to create a structure and system of excellence for them to work. I remember when I formed my team for D. E. Jackson Enterprises, LLC. I had gathered a wonderful group of professionals ranging from Accountants to Logistics experts and business administrators. Once I gathered them, I spent a lot of time discussing my visions, what I wanted to happen, and the system by which we would operate. I wanted us to establish an administrative structure that could manage the greatness of where the enterprise was heading. If we operated like a "Ma and Pop" business from the beginning, then that was all we could expect in terms of demand. I came out of the gate setting up systems, developing procedures, creating documentation, and placing checks and balances in line as if the enterprise was a multi-national, multi-million dollar corporation. When people of substance see you at your beginning with vision and courage to present your gift, product, idea, or concept in such a fashion, they will not only give you audience with them, but they will also give you opportunities on their level. But you cannot do this by yourself! You need people you can trust. You may be saying,

"Well, I do not have money to pay a staff." Neither did I, at first. You have to have people who believe in you and what you are doing to the point that they will volunteer their time and expertise until you can pay them.

The last tip I would offer is that you have to know when to accept and when to decline opportunities. Just because a door opened for you does not mean it is for you. The truth is that being too accessible and overly visible can decrease your value and demand. I was on a flight a couple of years ago and I was sitting next to an award-winning musician and his manager. Although he lived in Atlanta, he told me that he rarely played shows in his hometown. I asked him why. He told me that because people knew he lived in Atlanta, they did not value his performances as much as those who lived in other cities. So, staging shows too much in Atlanta was actually lowering his premium, which directly lowered his demand level. I have held on to this statement ever since I heard it and I hope you will, too. You cannot put your gift out there every time you get a chance to do so unless it will support and bolster your value. Sometimes, you have to say 'No, thank you'! This requires you to exercise self-control and manage the desire to be "desperate" for any moment that presents itself. When you know that you have something of value that people want, then you can wait patiently and wisely for the right moments to present themselves to you. Then you make your move—when the coast is clear for you.

So far, we have discussed extensively about discovering your purpose by knowing your gifts. Now, let us move on in our journey by talking about how to recognize when you have gotten into your room: the moment in time you have been waiting for to showcase your gifts to the world!

SECTION II

Recognizing that You Are in Your Room

"maketh room for him..."
(Psalm 18:16)

I hope that you have gained a deeper sense of the importance of knowing what your gifts are to experiencing true and sustained success in your purpose. If you are reading this book, I am confident that you are hardworking, ambitious, and determined to be all that God created you to be. You have made sacrifices, survived setbacks, endured hardship, and beat several odds all because you would not give up on your purpose. If you have had similar experiences like me, then you have had people tell you to your face that you would not be anything perhaps because you come from a humble background. Inversely, you may have come from a loving family environment that nurtured your gifts and provided you with support both emotionally and financially. However, you have hit some bumps in the road of life as you got older and now you feel like you are off track. You may have come to a crossroads in your life, where you recognize the need for a major shift and makeover of your life and work. All of these realities are valid and can lead you to push yourself to the next level and the next part of the overall journey to ultimate purpose. This type of mentality can create and cultivate a drive where you are constantly grinding with your head bowed low and eyes focused on your goals. This posture is necessary in many regards in order to remain steadfast and unyielding in your pursuit of destiny. However, sometimes, we can become so focused, so hardworking, so determined that we miss the fact that our hard work has actually paid off. We have made it to our "room."

Proverbs 18:16 suggests that when we present our gifts to the world as something of value, then the gift will make room for us. I understand room to mean your moment, opportunity, audience, platform, organization, or place for which your purpose is fully maximized. It is the place where purpose, compensation, and impact intersect in a meaningful way. It is the moment that you dreamed of happening and has now become a reality. It is a platform on which you saw your hero or mentor decades ago, and you worked diligently to prepare yourself for it. You have made it to the room. But do you realize that you are actually in your room? Have you been so busy grinding with blinders on such that you have not perceived that you actually made it there? An equally important question would be this: do you know the gift, strategy, and activity that got you to the room?

The reality is that if you do not know what gift is working for you, then you will walk into destiny without being aware of what has actually happened to you. And what will happen is that you will have a gift that has value and is recognized by amazing people who then open the door for you to come into the room, and now you are in the room. However, because you are not paying attention to the fact that you have shifted and transitioned due to your grinding mentality and you do not fully know what gift is working for you, then you will be in your moment and will not be impotent in the room. How many of you are in your moment right now standing there scratching your head saying, How did I get here? What has got me here? Beloved, you have been through too much stress, worked too hard, and have made tremendous sacrifices to get to your room and therefore should not be unable to truly work your room! When I say, 'work your room,' I mean to fully maximize your moment through the skillful combination of your gift, knowledge, experiences, and wisdom.

Pre, Current, and Post

When I was studying history in the Africana Studies Department at Cornell University, one of the ways we would categorize an occurrence would be to segment it into three categories: pre-, current, and post-. For instance, if we were discussing the impacts that civilization had on a group of people, we would examine the way the people were before civilization occurred (pre-civilization period), the way the people responded during civilization (civilization period), and the way the people changed, if so, after civilization (post-civilization period). Some people have a problem with this type of breakdown and I can see how it is challenging in terms of certain groups' history and control of telling their story. Nonetheless, in this discussion about recognizing that you are in your room, it can be a useful tool to you. You have to determine what the pre-room period, the room period, and the post-room period look like, will be like, and how you will be in each of these periods. This is important for at least three reasons.

The first reason is that your strategies shift based upon which period you are in. What it takes to get you to your room during the pre-room phase is different from the strategies you would use to transition from one room to a new one. It is essential for you to be able to assess your environment and adapt your strategies to properly fit what you are addressing and facing. The second reason is also based on a shifting. Your work ethic and focus also shift based on the period that you are in. When you are grinding and sacrificing before your moment in time, you are more focused on developing your gift, creating a track record of your ability, and figuring out how you are going to arrive at your destined place. When you actually arrive, you have to continue to work hard but it is in a different way. You are now focused on bringing together all that you have learned, experienced, and possessed to constantly be "on" or ready to be your absolute best in the room. When you have moved on to the next room, your work ethic is one of analyzing what you learned from the previous room and discerning what it will take to get to your next room. The reality is that what got you to the first room may not be the same thing that gets you to your next room.

The last reason why understanding these three periods is important is that who you are as a person—in terms of your personality and internal compass—adjusts based upon the period that you find yourself in. When you are in a pre-room phase, you are more driven and ambitious compared to when you are in the room. In the room, you are intentional, strategic, and in performance mode. Performance mode is when the lights and eyes are on you to see why you are in the room and what you plan to contribute to the space and field. Performance mode requires you to constantly be "on" and able to deliver the desired results consistently. This shifts your personality, how you care for yourself and your appearance. In your post-room period, you are in recovery and re-orientation mode. You are looking back over your experience in the room to learn the necessary lessons from both your victory and failures, your success and your losses. This is needed to assist you in your future endeavors. You also take time to catch up on lost sleep, reengage with friends and loved ones, and bandage yourself from the wounds you got from executing your gifts well. I will talk about this more. The re-orientation mode is about figuring out where your destination is, what your next moves are, and how you are going to get to your next room. But first things first—let us dig deeper into the heart of the matter for this section and that is realizing that you have made it to the place you have been working so hard to get to.

Recognizing that You Are in the Room

How do you know that you are in your room? This is a question that people who are serious about their purpose must ask themselves regularly. It is most beneficial to ask this question and prayerfully decide the answer to this before you get started working. This is why, as I discussed in Section I, you need to have a clearly written vision and mission statement that guides you towards your room and also lets you know how close you are to your moment of destiny. One of the challenges for many gifted people is that you get started working before you have determined what your destination is! If you start working without first determining this information, you will be expending energy, time, and resources without a guarantee of success. I like the way one of my covenant brothers described it in a sermon, Pastor Zichri Osler of Light of the World in Atlanta, GA. He said, in essence, that if you have not determined what a win or what success looks like for you, then you would work too hard and perhaps never accomplish your goals or work right past your goals.

Moreover, you must not only determine what indicators help you realize you are in the room, you also have to set markers along the way to let you know you are heading in the right direction and to give an estimate of how close you are! As I shared earlier, I have taken my fair share of road trips while in school. I have driven from New York to Atlanta and back a few times by myself. One of the things that helped me endure those long trips was to set benchmark cities. What I mean by that is that I knew it would take me three hours to get to a certain city and that was all I focused on, not the entire trip. This was helpful to me because thinking about the entire trip was overwhelming, but breaking it down into sections made the trip more manageable. Similarly, in your journey to destiny, you need to divide your trip into manageable sections to keep yourself on track with your purpose and provide accurate indicators that you are heading in the right direction. Another way to say this is that, successful people have strategically built their lives in phases. Rome was not built in a day. I can name numerous people in our history, who can testify to the fact that it took many years of hard work, struggle, and strategy to get to great success. It did not happen in one attempt. It is important to partner with God through prayer and study of the Word when setting these makers because what you decide is this—the sign that you made it may not be God's will.

While God will confirm His word with witnesses, signs, and wonders, we cannot build our lives on "signs" if we really want to experience consistent success in purpose. The main reason for this is that signs can fool you and contradict what God is saying. There is a great passage in Acts 27:9-14 where Paul is sailing to see Caesar and he advised the leaders of the ship not to continue sailing due to perceived danger ahead. But the centurion believed the master and owner of the ship more than Paul's word and continued sailing. Then, a "sign" came that the master of the ship was right while Paul was wrong as expressed in verse 13, *"And when the south wind blew softly, supposing that they had obtained their purpose, loosing thence, they sailed close by Crete."* The centurion assumed that the blowing south wind was a sort of confirmation that they should be sailing on but it was not. The next verse tells us that not long after they had set sail, violent windstorm came and almost destroyed the ship. I share this because you have to trust the original, overall word from God for your purpose and destiny more than you do signs. Signs should only confirm and support what God said, and not replace it. In addition to planning and setting markers for arriving at success, you have to pay attention to what life and your experiences are teaching and showing you.

Life Experiences Can Tell You

There are, at least, three things that your life's experience can tell you, to let you know that you have shifted from pre-room to the room.

Shift in Routine. When you realize that your old routine no longer works, then this is a sign that you need to reimagine your routine or that you have shifted to a new level and your gift has landed you in your room of destiny. I know you may be saying to yourself that you have been doing this like this for years and it worked but now it is not working and you are scratching your head, trying to figure out how the old way always got results before but it is not getting results now. Now you are in your room! You are in a new place; you are in a different space. I used to run a little track back in the day and I remember talking to people who were really gifted at track and field events about what made them run faster and performed better. One man shared with me that he used to train each summer in high terrain and altitude areas. I did not fully understand why this helped them. He said he trained in these high altitude areas because it is harder to breathe at higher altitudes. Therefore, the struggle and the desire to perform in a new place as you did in the old, familiar place would make you stronger. But you had to push past the resistance and discomfort to gain the benefits of the new environment. And the result would be that when he returned home, he would outperform everyone else because he had been training at a new height and level. I did not fully comprehend this lesson until I experienced altitude difference on a trip to Bolivia while I was a seminarian at Union in New York. Bolivia, South America is one of the highest places in South America. Once we landed in La Paz, I could barely breathe when I got off the plane but as I continued to push and function, I adjusted to the higher altitude. Therefore, if you find yourself in a space where it is difficult to breathe, then maybe it is a sign that you are at a higher level, in a different room, in your moment. Your natural response may be to run away from this new place or resist the pressure. I want to encourage you to not fight the strain in breathing but rather just go through it so God can condition you for the new level.

New Challenges and Obstacles. Another way you know that you are in your room is that you are facing new challenges, obstacles, and problem. When you make it into your room, you will see things that you have never seen before and it can be shocking and stressful at first. I do not know about you but in the last year, I have seen stuff I have never seen before. You look at your new surrounding and say, 'Wow, I did not know that these types of things can actually happen to a person. I did not know that this stuff actually happens.' I want to assure you that these challenges and obstacles are not an indication that you are out of the will of God. It is quite the opposite, beloved. It is often an indication that you are on a new level because we know as the old adage says, "With every new level, there are new devils." While this is true, I want to caution you not to live your life looking for a devil under every rock. Not everything you face is from the adversary of your souls. Yet if you continue to rebuke and name every single obstacle, challenge, or resistance you face as the enemy, then you could cancel out the very experiences that are designed to train you to excel in the new level. Then you begin to wonder why you are having problems surviving on the new level. You have called preparation the devil and rebuked it, and in essence caused the help of God to be nullified. The reality is that some of the things you are experiencing right now have not come to stop or destroy you but rather to make you aware that you have been elevated, and to prepare you for the greatness of your moment. Never forget the promise we have in Isaiah 54:17 that *"No weapon formed against you shall prosper!"*

Along the same lines of recognizing new obstacles is also realizing that you have new "enemies" or "haters" you have not had before. I mention this with some reticence because unfortunately, we live in a culture that is overly focused on haters and enemies. I have experienced personally and firsthand how being connected with people who are living with a mentality that assumes everyone is against you and only want to see the worst in you can negatively affect all of your connection and relationships. Nonetheless, it cannot be denied that there are people who do not like your progression and do not want to see you become successful. I remember seeing a statement on Facebook a while back that was so powerful. It suggested that sometimes you might not even know that you have arrived at the next level until the people that are on the level above you begin to hate or dislike you. I am sure you have had people who seemed to have more material things than you have, more education, or a seemingly better life, yet they cannot withstand you or attempt to sabotage your efforts. It can baffle you if you recognize that this is happening. Well, my friend, open your eyes and recognize that those who were once above you are now your equals! They are threatened by the fact that you have got to their level and want to convince you that you do not belong in your room. People may have things, titles, positions, and influence but this does not mean they are secure in themselves or their accomplishments. But when they see you walking in confidence and security, they will be frightened because they know that if you get what they have in addition to the inner assurance you already have, then you will surpass them in no time. Remember that most people, regardless of how nice or mean they are, tend to be territorial and will fight to maintain their dominance in their territory. So some of you are crying to God and asking why certain people hate you. Why are these people blocking me? Why are these people trying to set me up? The word of the Lord to you beloved is to dry your eyes and rejoice because this attack from haters is one of the best things that could ever signify that you are worth a "good thing" in that room. It confirms that you are on a higher level because people do not fight people on lower levels but rather they fight at their level. Rejoice because you have been elevated. Here is a prayer I learned from Numbers 10:35 that has helped me to clear my room of the haters in any new territory: *"And it came to pass, when the ark set forward, that Moses said, Rise up, LORD, and let thine enemies be scattered; and let them that hate thee flee before thee."* This was the prayer that Moses prayed for the children of Israel after two years of being in the wilderness in Mt. Sinai before they set forward again for the promise land. He knew they would be traveling through foreign lands and would face new enemies and haters. Nonetheless, if the LORD (Jehovah/Yahweh) would stand up and go before them, He Himself would clear the way of haters and enemies so that once they made entry into new places, the struggle would be easy to conquer. I pray this prayer every morning before I start my day, facing in all four directions; and it is amazing how effective this prayer is. I want to caution you before you start praying these words because it may shock you to realize those whom God may scatter and cause to flee from your life. Yes, it may be people that you thought were your friends, supports, and allies. It may even be family members.

Elevation in Value. I had a very embarrassing but telling experience about a year ago, which informed me that I was on a new level where my words and actions had value. I was asked to be a part of a big forum at a local college. While standing on the side, I was having what I thought was a private conversation with some colleagues and made a statement thinking I was speaking to my colleagues, but there were some college students who overheard my statements. At the end of the event, I was asked to step into a room with these students and they began to say, "We heard what you said." Did you say it? I said yes because I have learned not to lie as much as possible. They proceeded to share with me about how my statements bothered them, considering my professions. These incredibly brilliant young men began to share their sincere feelings, and all I could do was stand there and say, "You are right, and I apologize. Here is my card. If I can do anything to help you, please let me know." See, there is a price for not recognizing that you have shifted to another level. When you are elevated, so do the value of your words and actions. People are now watching and listening to you, though they never did before. Your inability to realize this shift can cost you success and longevity in your room. If this happens to you, own your mistake, do not deny it. Apologize and move forward.

I must be honest and tell you that I was so embarrassed and grieved that this happened to me. As I continued to reflect on this event, I heard the voice of God say to me to not grieve over this but rather rejoice! I was somewhat puzzled at these words because I could not see anything to rejoice about so I asked, "Father why?" He said, 'Because this situation came to make you aware that you are on an entirely new level to the point that you cannot just say what you feel like saying because in people's hearing, it has value now. Furthermore, be glad that this happened early in your journey rather than later when your misguided statements could cause you to be removed from the level. By it happening early in the game, you have very little to lose, but some pride.' I do not know whom this word may be for. Perhaps the enemy may be coming against you right now and you do not understand why they are coming in such a manner, and the pressure is causing you to feel like running away from your new place and causing you to have self-doubt if you should be in your room, in the first place. But thanks be unto God that despite the haters and resistance, He has raised you up and given you the power to stand through the pressure. A valuable key to success is to ignore the haters and push past embarrassment and failure. You have to learn how not to be emotionally involved in the process of success attainment. Simply clear the room and work it!

From Carrying Purpose to Activating Purpose

This discussion about recognizing that you are in your room is so important because people who are gifted have been so a long time. You have been living and functioning in places that could not handle your gift and greatness, yet life brought you through this route for character building, life lessons, and strength training. When you are in the pre-room phase, you are simply carrying purpose, gift, and greatness. You are not necessarily able to fully activate and manifest it. You do so in bits and pieces, as needed and when appropriate. However, when you get into your room, this is the time to shift from carrying your purpose to fully activating your purpose. I remember when I became a Senior Pastor. I had to shift from carrying the word to activating the word every week. Before pastoring, I was not preaching regularly. I taught small groups, trained leaders, and worked in administration and pastoral care. Nonetheless, I had tremendous skills and gifts as a communicator of God's word, though I was not regularly using them. But once I was put in my room as the Senior Pastor of a historic church, I had to activate that oratory ability. Let me tell you, it was an adjustment because I had been conditioned to being one way, of which I was hiding and being selective of when I showed my gift and to having the freedom and authority to fully manifest my gift so that I could work the room that I had worked so hard to get to. It reminds me of my biblical namesake, King David.

David had been anointed by Prophet Samuel to be the second king of Israel years before he actually became king (See 1 Samuel 16). Many of you have already been gifted and anointed for your room years before you actually got to your room. However, the process of getting from the call to the manifestation can be tough. David was a fugitive, as Bishop Jackie McCullough describes him in a sermon of hers, On the Run from Saul. Can you imagine how difficult it must have been to still hold on to the words of Samuel that one day he would be what God said he would be. You have to hold on to your dreams and never lose sight of the room God promised you despite the obstacles, attacks, and delays. If God spoke it, showed it, or revealed it to you, then you can depend on it. God's word cannot and will never return to Him void but it will accomplish its goal in your life (Isaiah 55:11). In order to keep your dream alive and to keep your fervor in your gift, He will give you practice in transition. When David was hiding in the cave of Adullam, God reminded David, 'Although you are on the run for your life and it seems that you may not live long enough to become King, I will confirm your destiny' (See 1 Samuel 22). God allowed me in the hundreds of count to find David in the cave who connected to him. David was able to take men from messed-up backgrounds and problem-filled lives and transform them into a band of loyal fighters. David was in his pre-room experience, but it was so necessary to help him prepare for the room of being the King. It was not until he was anointed king for the second time at Hebron after the death of Saul and then the third time in Jerusalem to unite Israel and Judah as a joint kingdom that he was able to shift from his pre-room stage to the room. Can you imagine the process that David had to go through to transition in his mentality, demeanor, and practices—from being a shepherd to a vagabond and then to a King over a united kingdom! If it had not been for the experience in the wilderness and the cave, then David would not have been able to work his room.

Overview of Section II

Section I was designed to help you recognize the gifts that brought you to your room. Now, the goal of Section II is to get you to accept that you are actually in the room. In Section II, we will discuss Principles 4, 5, and 6. Principle 4 is "Acknowledging Your Moment is Equally Important to Knowing Your Gift." This is so vital because if you know your gift without recognizing that you are in your room or moment, then you will be in your room but impotent. Principle 5 is "Keep the Old and New in Proper Perspective." One of the biggest enemies to purpose is using old methods and strategies in a new place. This principle will show you how to make the proper transition in order to work your room. Principle 6 is "Preparation Starts before the Room, Not in the Room." This principle is absolutely essential to working your room because your commitment to preparation will affect the timing of reaching the place where purpose is manifested. Your lack of preparation can also hinder your performance in your room.

PRINCIPLE 4

Acknowledging Your Moment is Equally Important to Knowing Your Gifts

Proverbs 18:16 is clear that when a person makes the decision to present their dominant gift as a valuable asset to the world, great people will make room for the individual. This room then places the person next to or in front of other great people, thereby providing the atmosphere to manifest God's purpose for his/her life. So you cannot expect to be in front of great people and fully operate in your destiny if you are not brought into the room. This is why it is important to devote as much attention to your room as you do to your gift. What is the point of having a great gift if you cannot use it to manifest God-given destiny in your life to the glory of God. Gifts have to operate somewhere. They are not being displayed or used just for the sake of it. The gift God gave you, which will usher you into destiny, needs a stage, a place and an audience in order for it to be effectual. My concern is that many gifted people have worked so hard on their gift and have given very little strategic and intentional thought to their room. I want to dig into this ideal in greater depth here to help you balance out your focus so that your hard work in the areas of gift development will not go to waste in the room of your purpose.

Room Defined

When we look closer at the word "room" in Proverbs 18:16, it really provides a powerful understanding to how God progresses people closer and securely into destiny. The word "room" comes from a Hebrew word that means "to grow wide or large." It suggests that a space that was once one size has come to a point where it must enlarge itself to accommodate an increase. I love this concept of room in the text as it pertains to your purpose. This means that the place that God has prepared for you to move into might not look like it has enough space to accommodate you but at the appointed time, it will enlarge itself to allow you to enter and not feel crowded in the new space. This new and enlarged space will manifest itself in your life as your moment, your platform, your audience, your groove, your flow, your set place, or your due season. This is indeed a Kingdom understanding or divine placement into your purpose, which crushes the world's crab-in-the-bucket mentality.

Plenty Good Room

See, many people feel that there are limited resources, spaces, and opportunities in the world. Therefore, once you get what they think belongs to them, then they fight to keep you from "taking" their title, position, influence, or territory. Your entrance into the room sends them into instant defense mode because you are a perceived threat. But the reality is that God has the power to enlarge the territory to make enough room for you and anyone else that is there. Most people who are intimidated by you in the room either are about to be cast out of the room or were not placed in the room by godly means in the first place. Many people feel like they could lose their place in the room due to their insecure and low self-view because they seduced, manipulated, and intimidated people before they could get to their present space. As a result, they are willing to lie, set up, and engage in carnal tactics to maintain their place and remove potential threats. This was the problem with King Saul once he realized that David had the grace and gift to come into the room called "King." I can imagine Saul wondering how David could be king when he, himself, was already king. In 1 Samuel 18:5-8 NKJV it states:

> *So David went out wherever Saul sent him, and behaved wisely. And Saul set him over the men of war, and he was accepted in the sight of all the people and also in the sight of Saul's servants. Now it had happened as they were coming home, when David was returning from the slaughter of the Philistines, that the women had come out of all the cities of Israel, singing and dancing, to meet King Saul, with tambourines, with joy, and with musical instruments. So the women sang as they danced, and said: "Saul has slain his thousands, And David his ten thousands." Then Saul was very angry, and the saying displeased him; and he said, "They have ascribed to David ten thousands, and to me they have ascribed only thousands. Now what more can he have but the kingdom?" So Saul eyed David from that day forward.*

This story reflects the world's view of addition versus the Kingdom perspective, very well. Saul saw David's victory in war as a removal of him from the kingdom but David's success in the room of military actually made Saul look good even though David had surpassed Saul in military victory. How was that so? Well, notice that the women did not acknowledge David first, but rather Saul. They gave respect to Saul as being the one to set the standard for what getting victory against the enemy looked like.

However, now that David was appointed to that position, he was experiencing exponential success in warfare. The people could see it and were not afraid to say it. However, Saul did not see that David's success was not a threat to his kingdom. Rather, out of his own insecurity and carnality, Saul began to view David as a threat and ultimately attempted to kill David and try to prevent him from moving into his destiny. But I want you to know that when God has purposed you to be, have or do something for the Kingdom, then no weapon formed against you shall prosper as promised in Isaiah 54:17. Some of you may be enduring attacks for being gifted in your room but let me encourage you to stand in the power of Christ as Ephesians 6:10-11 NKJV declares: *"Finally, my brethren, be strong in the Lord and in the power of His might. Put on the whole armor of God, that you may be able to stand against the wiles of the devil."*

As the old songwriter said decades ago, "There is plenty good room!" Remember that you do not have to compete with other people or be threatened by people with similar abilities and skills and who are in the room with you. No one can work the room like you can and you cannot work the room like they can. Be comfortable with your gift and stay in your lane. In addition, do not be intimidated or pushed out of the room because of insecure people who are threatened by your presence in the room. If they cannot see that there is plenty good room for all of you, then they are not Kingdom people and you need to deal with them as such. Be professional and courteous but do not connect yourself with them beyond the tasks at hand. They will be plotting to stop you but it will not work. Stay focused and work your room. I want to teach you a tool I have in my arsenal that has helped me stay focused and clear my room of unnecessary negative forces.

A Prayer to Clear Your Room

Allow me to share a prayer principle that will help you in your room if you face haters and enemies. (I mentioned this prayer earlier, but allow me to go deeper into it.) I am a witness that it will clear your room out so fast and effectively that it may startle you initially. I first heard this prayer taught by my spiritual father, the late Bishop Wilbert McKinley and have taken it with me around the world. I continue to get testimonies of its effects from people who believe in the word of the LORD and his messenger. It comes from Numbers 10:35 NKJV and says *"So it was, whenever the ark set out, that Moses said: "Rise up, O LORD! Let Your enemies be scattered, And let those who hate You flee before You."* This is the prayer that Moses prayed when the LORD spoke to him to move the children of Israel from Mount Sinai in the wilderness further in their journey towards the Promise Land. They had been out of Egypt for two years and now it was time to continue the journey. As they moved, they would definitely enter into foreign and enemy territories. As they moved forward, they would face people who saw them as a threat on their land or "room." So to reduce warfare, strife, and delay, Moses declared these words to make the way clear for them. This prayer then is for people who have a covenant relationship with God and are moving on a promise from God.

Covenant here means that you have a contract relationship with God. That comes for Christian believers by grace through faith in Jesus Christ, which comes by way of repentance and belief. One thing about covenant that is connected to this topic is that when God makes a covenant with you, He also makes promises to you. When God formed a covenant with Abram in Genesis 12, He made promises that all the families of the Earth will be blessed through Abram. So when you have a relationship of righteousness with God and are walking by faith in the promises of God for your life, then you do not allow haters, enemies, dissenters, witches/warlocks, jealous people, or those who want to bring up your past intimidate you in your room. You simply take your Kingdom covenant rights and authority and ask God to move opposition out of your way.

When Moses had prepared everyone for the move, he said first, "Rise up, O LORD." The ancient Israelites understood God to be the King of kings and ultimate ruler of the universe who sat upon His throne, lifted and glorious in power. When Moses said *rise up*, he was saying, *Please sir, stand up and give us an assurance that you are fully engaged in our progress.* The representation of the LORD's presence was the Ark of the Covenant. The Ark was the tangible proof that God Himself was among them. And whenever the Ark moved, it was as if God moved ahead. So, in essence, Moses was saying, "As we move the Ark, stir up and let your Shekinah glory or manifested presence show forth." There is nothing more rewarding and comforting than knowing that God is not only with us but fully engaged in making our movement successful. That is why Moses addressed God as LORD! When you see the word "LORD" in all capital letters, it is the covenant name of God. This is the One who is self-existent and self-contained. He does not need anything outside of Himself to exist, function, or execute His wishes. Everything He needs is contained within His being. As a result, He makes promises, remembers His promises, has what it takes within Himself to fulfill His promises and at the appointed time, He will make good and fulfill His promises to His people. Another benefit to God standing up was that He was big enough to see far ahead. The LORD knew what was coming down the road and would then provide guidance and strategy to the people as they moved so that they would not be ambushed or caught unawares by anything coming ahead. You do not have to progress into any room blind and unaware of what you are about to face. God will reveal it to you by His spirit through so many ways. Ask the LORD to stand up on your trip so He can make you aware of what is ahead and how to address it.

Then Moses went on to make a distinction between enemies and haters. He asked the LORD to scatter enemies but cause haters to flee. Note that Moses described the people he would encounter on his journey as the enemies and haters of God. The push back and underhanded tactics you may be experiencing in your room are not your concern or situation to deal with. They are pushing back against the LORD Himself. The reason I say this is that it is the will of God that you are who you are and moving into where you are going. Never forget that you being in your room at the moment is the predestined will of God for you and all of your existence. So any person, place, or thing that tries to block or uproot that is coming against God and not you. Therefore, remove yourself from this situation emotionally and mentally and give it to the LORD to handle. Remember that the battle is not yours but the LORD's.

Moses makes a distinction between enemies and haters because they are different. Enemies were those people who were easy to recognize as such because they were clearly different from the Israelites. You know an enemy because they are clearly opposite of what you represent as a person of God. They have glaringly opposing philosophies, practices, and tactics than you have as a Kingdom person. You can spot an enemy a mile away and they have no problem identifying themselves as your enemy. Moses says that those people are to be scattered. This means, "LORD, please keep your enemies disjointed, out of the same area, and without the ability to ever united together against your people." What a terrible experience if all of your past and present enemies were to unite together to attack you. Wow! But thanks be to God that when you declare this prayer, God will cause them to be spread out all over the place and out of your path of movement. Moreover, He will destroy any plans to bring them together and thwart any secret plot to rise up against you as a joint force. Now how enemies are handled is very different from how haters are because haters are harder to identify.

Hate is an emotion of intense or passionate dislike for someone or something. Hatred is a deep and powerful feeling that can drive people to do distasteful and evil things if not addressed. The most dangerous aspect of hate is that you can have people around you who appear to be for you, support you and believe in your dreams and yet they have hatred in their heart for you and your purpose. Some of you are in relationship with, related to, working with, or sitting with a hater right now. Haters, Moses declares, must flee before the presence of the LORD. This suggests keeping haters constantly moving and never able to settle down. Once a hater reaches a place along your path of movement, let them be unable to gain stability or tenure in that place and push them onto another place. As for persons who pretend to be your friends and support with secret intentions to destroy you while you are engaged in your God-given destiny, they forfeit the benefit of stability and longevity! I must put Psalm 37:1-15 here! I know this is a long passage but I want you to see how seriously God takes His actions against wicked people who try to come against His people who are actively engaged in their Kingdom covenant purpose:

> *Fret not thyself because of evildoers, neither be thou envious against the workers of iniquity. For they shall soon be cut down like the grass, and wither as the green herb. Trust in the Lord, and do good; so shalt thou dwell in the land, and verily thou shalt be fed. Delight thyself also in the Lord: and he shall give thee the desires of thine heart. Commit thy way unto the Lord; trust also in him; and he shall bring it to pass. And he shall bring forth thy righteousness as the light, and thy judgment as the noonday. Rest in the Lord, and wait patiently for him: fret not thyself because of him who prospereth in his way, because of the man who bringeth wicked devices to pass. Cease from anger, and forsake wrath: fret not thyself in any wise to do evil. For evildoers shall be cut off: but those that wait upon the Lord, they shall inherit the earth. For yet a little while, and the wicked shall not be: yea, thou shalt diligently consider his place, and it shall not be. But the meek shall inherit the earth; and shall delight themselves in the abundance of peace. The wicked plotteth against the just, and gnasheth upon him with his teeth. The Lord shall laugh at him: for he seeth that his day is coming. The*

wicked have drawn out the sword, and have bent their bow, to cast down the poor and needy, and to slay such as be of upright conversation. Their sword shall enter into their own heart, and their bows shall be broken.

Now, I want to return your attention back to Numbers 10:35, which can actually work in your daily life. I pray this prayer every day in all four directions so that I am covered all around. You never know which direction God will take you each day so you want to be prepared. However, one disclaimer I like to give people before this prayer is this: Do not be surprised when you see someone ends up leaving your life! You might be shocked and heartbroken to discover that someone close to you or that you loved was an enemy or hater all along. You will be jolted to see how quickly supervisors, co-workers, relatives, and other people begin to clear out of your way and your life. We are human; so you are expected to have whatever response comes natural to you. Express it and experience the emotion. Once you get done, get yourself back on track, refocus and keep moving forward! This is essential because you have to remain in a position whereby you can always discern God's timing and openings to you up ahead.

Discerning a Window of Opportunity

Discernment is a powerful spiritual tool given to Kingdom people by the Holy Spirit. It helps you to know the source, purpose, and manifestation of things whether it be divine, demonic, or human in origin and expression. Without discernment, you can make connections with haters or move too fast in making decisions that could cost you money, time, or your reputation. Furthermore, without discernment, you could be ushered into a room and you do not recognize that you have come into your moment, platform, or audience. It is vitally important that you are constantly aware when God has shifted you into a new season and level. Honestly, this is easier said than done because sometimes God will shift you and you do not have a clue about the development due to your overly focused investment in gifts. But the wisdom and sensitivity of the Spirit gives you the knowledge that you are not where you were.

This is an important aspect of recognizing your moment or room. You have to be able to discern when a window of opportunity has been opened for you. God will open moments of opportunities and you have to be able to discern that this is a door that has been opened to you so you can seize the moment. Otherwise, you will miss it. And there is no guarantee that this exact moment with the exact same configuration will reappear to you again. Now, you are destined to get to the place where God wants for you. I encourage you, however, to take advantage of the doors and windows He opens the first time so that you can avoid unneeded and unwanted delays, battle wounds, and stress. Do not get me wrong, you will go through obstacles, challenges, and pain but it is needed to build character in you. But when you miss windows of opportunities, you delay your progression but God will open another door. Again, this new window or door will not be like the previous, so seize the moment presented the first time.

With that said, trust God's leading and not your own understanding as given in Proverbs 3:5-6. When you are led by ambition, feelings, and impatience, you will jump into "windows" and "doors," calling it God and it may be a trap and set up. There is a delicate balance in terms of discerning windows of opportunities. Just because it opens does not mean it is from God nor does it mean it is for you right now. Keeping your written goals and vision statement in front of you as a guidance measure will aid you tremendously in discerning if this moment is for you at this particular time. If you discern that this window is indeed from the Lord and meant for you to move into now, then move with intention. Sometimes, gifted people miss a moment by spending too much time trying to figure out if they should move or how they should move. Again, when you have had some discernment by prayer, comparison of events or situations with your mission, and through wise counsel from your multitude of advisors (make sure you have surrounded yourself with a time-tested and trusted group of people who can help you discern and discuss your journey to purpose), move through the window with immediate effect. Not only do you not want to miss this moment but you also do not know how long this window will be open for you. Only God knows the reason He opens the door, so get in your room and work it! Sometimes, you have to trust your gut feelings in moving forward into your room.

Trust Your Gut Feelings

I have learned from experience that it is important to follow your gut feeling in most cases. Proverb 20:27 tells us, *"The spirit of man is the candle of the LORD, searching all the inward parts of the belly."* The LORD does speak often from our belly partly because when we think of where the Holy Spirit would dwell in the human body, most folks would say the stomach or belly. The reason for this is that when we think of a part of the body that the majority of people would first associate with being "filled" or "full," it would be the belly. As a result, if we make ourselves more sensitive to the sensation and moving of the Spirit as discerned and experienced from our belly, we can get direction. The primary feeling we should get in our gut when discerning if we should move forward or not is peace!

Peace is an indication of God's approval on a matter. When you lack peace about something, God is speaking to you to reconsider, delay, or abandon all together. Often times, we ignore, question, or discount what the Lord may be saying to us through our core being because it did not come to us in some super spiritual, spooky, or overly obvious way. We allow our intellect, emotions, and fear to block us from doing what we know we need to do. As a result, we stay in situations, jobs, relationships, locations, habits, and other things for days, weeks, months, and yes years, even beyond what our gut tells us; and then we wonder why we land in a place of stagnation and frustration. Beloved, I want to challenge you to add your Spirit-led gut feelings to your bag of discernment for success in your purpose. I do not want you to miss your moment by having your window of opportunities closed on you because you would not listen to and follow the Spirit speaking to your from your belly. There is something, however, that can help support your gut feeling in a more concrete way.

Glimpses of the Room in Your Pre-Room

In the introduction part of Section II, I talked about how it is important to determine from the beginning what your room looks like. A strategy that can help you discern if you have made it to your room is to pay attention and remember all of your experiences during your time of preparation. These experiences often provides a glimpse of your future room before you actually get there physically. This glimpse becomes a photographic marker in your mind and heart that will send a pulse of confirmation into your soul that you have arrived at what you only peeked into from your past experiences. This has distinct benefits in this regard. One benefit of holding onto future glimpses is that it gives you the strength to hold on to the truth of what your room is in the face of struggle and deception. When you are on the journey to your destiny, you will face trials, disappointments, and a struggle. Again, it is all a necessary part of the process; however, when you have something to hold onto, which can give you hope and assurance in spite of your present circumstances, you will reach your goal if you keep walking and trusting God.

Furthermore, life will allow people, offers, opportunities, and places to emerge on your path, which will look, sound, and feel like it is from God, and they all appear to form the pathway to the room that God has destined for you. Unfortunately, these "doors" can bamboozle ambitious, gifted people because they open so quickly and easily. It offers everything you want at a seemingly quick rate with less work or investment. It is exactly what you want and how you want it. So, when you have gotten real and authentic glimpse of what your moment, platform, impact, and audience really is, then you will face situations that tend to get you seduced and pulled off track through counterfeits and deterrent opportunities. I remember getting a glimpse of my future in law enforcement before I started my training at the Police Academy. My experience was filled with joys, difficulties, and struggle. Some days, the only thing I had to hold myself on track and to keep me motivated to get to my room was the glimpse I got months before being hired by the department. I had a similar experience when I was a student in college.

I was a student leader then and was often invited to represent the university at meetings. I was selected to go to a particular meeting in New York City and had the privilege of staying at one of the Ivy League Clubs. Although it was not the Cornell Club, it was a very life-transforming experience for me. I remember going to dinner that first evening alone and sitting in the dining room, looking at Grand Central Station. I had an open-air vision of me sitting at numerous formal dinners and entertaining diplomats, marketplace leaders, and social transformers. I was so overwhelmed with emotions and awe that I called my dear Queen Mother and told her that I had just had a glimpse of myself sitting at the Penn Club. Now, over a decade later, that glimpse has given me the courage and tenacity to endure hardship and turbulence to land in many rooms that have afforded me the opportunity to entertain the people I saw in my vision. I am sure that many of you have also had some experiences that have shown you who you are going to be despite where you currently are today. Store those memories in a treasure box in your mind. They will come in handy when the going gets tough.

The second benefit to having glimpses is that it instills a more realistic view of what your room will be like. Most gifted people are dreamers and creative, possessing vivid imaginations. When you think about your room, I am sure you have amazing concepts and ideas of what it will be and what you want it to be. More than likely, your thoughts of your future room is a romantic one and not yet an experienced one. When I say romantic, I mean it is perfect, ideal, and neat as you have created it to be. However, the real experience may be nothing like what you have created it to be in your mind. Therefore, when some people actually make it into their moment and room, they are crushed and, in some ways, paralyzed due to the shock and disappointment. This is why some people tend to over-focus on their gifts and not the moment because they are more realistically acquainted with what they possess to work their room than they are with what the room actually looks like.

One of the best ways to address that disconnect between what you imagine the room to be and what it actually may be—beyond receiving a spiritual vision, trance, or dream—is exposure. Exposure is so valuable because it allows you to go to places, look at things, and get mentors and role models who are already in the room you are called to go and who will give you access to that room before you get there. I am reminded of the story of the transfiguration in St. Matthew 17 where Jesus gives three of his closest disciples, James, Peter, and John, a glimpse into a future room during their pre-room state, to help them in their post-room reality of crucifixion. I sincerely believe that if James, Peter, and John had not had the opportunity to see unequivocally that Jesus was truly who He said He was, including the fulfillment of the Law (Moses) and the Prophets (Elijah), then they would not have recovered from the shock and endured hard times as quickly and successfully as they did in the days of Jesus' crucifixion, burial, and resurrection. Moreover, the vitality of their ministry after the ascension of Christ was exceptional and far reaching in comparison to their fellow apostolic brethren that were not on the Mount of Transfiguration. And I would assert that the heavenly glimpse they had on the mountain left such an indelible mark on their souls and fueled the success of their ministry as soon as they were fully commissioned and empowered to work the room of their apostleship and bishopric.

As I shared earlier in the book, my childhood aspiration was to become a physician. I had so many romantic and idealistic views of what working in a hospital was like and what treating sick patients would feel like. It was not until I did a summer program at a prominent medical school in Virginia the summer after my Freshman year at Cornell that I had a real encounter with being a physician. I was rotating through the Emergency room shadowing neurosurgeons because that is what I thought I wanted to be. Well, I must say that after about three visits with these brilliant and young neurosurgeons, I quickly determined that neurosurgery and emergency medicine was not my forte. And honestly, deep down inside I knew that medicine in general was not my God-given purpose. It took me about another whole year or so to fully embrace it and make the necessary shift into destiny. I am so thankful for that eye-opening experience now because I was able to get on track with my purpose before investing years of hard study, finances, and effort in a field that was not truly aligned with my ultimate purpose. Nonetheless, that experience did provide an experience that I was able to transfer over to my calling of "preaching, teaching, and counseling." I learned that you have to begin developing the mentality of the place you want to go years before you actually get there.

Developing Room Mentality

Many of you reading this can agree that the big part of success in your purpose is your mentality. Success is not totally dependent on your gift, your intellect, your connections, or your work ethics. All of these things I just mentioned are birthed out of your mentality. You can have all of these things working for you but if you have a poor mentality or a narrow perspective about your purpose, it will directly affect when and how you enter the room of destiny. The truth of the matter is that the way you govern yourself in the room will be based on how you see yourself, your gifts, and your preparedness. When you go into your room, you have to act like you are in front of great people. You have to be poised and confident because you have been divinely and strategically positioned to work that room. Therefore, you must take ownership of the room and space. You have been waiting for this! You have been praying for it and struggling to get here. Why get to your moment and not maximize this opportunity (or as I keep saying, work your room) because your perspective and mentality is not on par with your gifts and work ethics? It is my purpose to coach and support you through this book so that you will be well prepared to the point that when you reach your room (and some of you are already in your room), you will not fumble but excel, progress, and work the space with a striking excellence.

I call it "Room Mentality." Room mentality is a mindset that reflects the values, practices, and culture of the place of your destiny. Each room, platform, venture, and audience has a culture and flow that is governed by spoken and unspoken rules and behaviors. Your success in the room hinges on your knowing and demonstrating these values quickly, correctly, and excellently. But again, in order to do that, you have to practice now. Some of you said, "Well, when I get there, I will do this and when I get there, I will do that." I must be honest and tell you that that mentality will not work. Practice makes perfect and is essential to building the right mentality. Practice helps you work out the kinks and errors before you get in your room. This must happen because when you walk into your moment and onto the stage, you cannot afford to make a whole lot of novice mistakes. You have to be almost flawless in the room to take hold of it at the beginning.

This is a hard saying but I care enough about your purpose to tell you such a truth. Some of you have been lamenting about your slow progress. You have been asking God why has this not happened yet for me. I thought I was making all of the right moves, developing my gift, and making the right connections. Yet, things have not manifested for me as I imagined them to. Perhaps, one of the reasons some of you have been delayed from entering your room is not because God has denied you access to it but because He is protecting your future by not allowing you get into your room under-prepared and thus potentially sabotage your moment. Please, get serious about preparing and fine-tuning your mentality. Besides, if your mindset is not in tune with destiny, then you will always over-focus on gifts and overlook the need to consciously work the room, thus placing you on a never-ending cycle of waiting for God to open the door while He waits on you to open your eyes and realize that you are already in the room. Now WORK YOUR ROOM TO THE GLORY OF GOD!

PRINCIPLE 5

Keep the Old and New in Proper Perspective

Anyone who knows me well knows that I LOVE TO DANCE. I dance everywhere, be it at the grocery store, on the street, and most certainly at church. Dancing is a way for me to demonstrate that I appreciate life and all that is happening in my life. However, as life's journey has elevated me to a higher level, I have noticed that I do not have the same liberties to dance as freely in public as I once did. There are expectations about how I should conduct myself as a public, social, and religious leader. This may have been what Michal, daughter of King Saul and wife of King David, thought about her husband's behavior when he successfully returned the Ark of the Covenant back to Jerusalem. Let us see what 2 Samuel 6:16, 20-23 NKJV says:

> *Now as the ark of the LORD came into the City of David, Michal, Saul's daughter, looked through a window and saw King David leaping and whirling before the LORD; and she despised him in her heart...Then David returned to bless his household. And Michal the daughter of Saul came out to meet David, and said, "How glorious was the king of Israel today, uncovering himself today in the eyes of the maids of his servants, as one of the base fellows shamelessly uncovers himself!" So David said to Michal, "It was before the LORD, who chose me instead of your father and all his house, to appoint me ruler over the*

*people of the LORD, over Israel. Therefore I
will play music before the LORD. And I will
be even more undignified than this, and will be
humble in my own sight. But as for the
maidservants of whom you have spoken, by
them I will be held in honor." Therefore
Michal the daughter of Saul had no children
to the day of her death.*

I have always found this story very interesting on a
number of levels. It can be inferred that David had a free
lifestyle of praising God before he became the King. This was
his old way of being before he was elevated into a new life of
royalty. David did not know this new way, for he was a
shepherd boy from a poor family, and neither did he attach
any dignity to his new position in God's presence. He just
wanted to be himself everywhere he went. The only person
who really taught him Palace etiquette was his friend
Jonathan. Therefore, Michal's response to David's behavior
was a clash of old and new, low class and high class, tradition
and progression. You may say that neither King David nor I
should care about what people think, especially about our
public actions—in terms of dancing. And in a measure, you
may be right. King David certainly thought so as we saw from
his response to Michal.

On the other hand, there is a need to understand that
perception becomes many people's realities. If people
perceive that you do not have the decorum, mannerism, or
maturity level to match the room that your gifts have brought
you into, then it can be assumed that you do not belong in the
room. I submit to you that balance is the key to life in
everything. How does one maintain the great qualities from

the last level and merge them successfully to the new level without compromising either part?

Gifted people must constantly remember the fact that when much has been given, much is required. A part of that requirement is showing the qualities and characteristics that go along with leadership. The same applies to you who serve as leaders in your homes, neighborhoods, faith communities, and organizations. People are looking up to you for guidance, inspiration, and direction; and their perception of you and your actions affects how they view you and respond to you. In the same breath, you have to find safe spaces and trustworthy people that will allow you to display the fullness of who you are. Having these places and people will help you balance out your life in amazing and healthy ways.

Another way to express my sentiment here is to say that you have to know what to show, when to show it, and to whom to show it. That is what I mean by keeping both the old and the new in perspective. You bring all of you to the room with the wisdom to know what needs to be shown now. Just because you are in your room now does not mean that you have to abandon everything about you before you got there. However, because you are on a new level and in a new place, you have to quickly discern and determine what you bring into the room and how you bring it. In order to work your room successfully, you have to embrace wholeheartedly that concept of putting your best foot forward. This means that you are displaying that polished, well organized, and sharply executed part of yourself and gift in your moment. In order to do this, you also have to understand the culture and expectation of the room. With that said, with ease and clarity, you can then manifest the appropriate aspects of your gifting and personality in the room in such a way that you are both authentic and effective. One's inability to do so can cause hindrances to one's progress on the next level.

Allow me to continue telling you about my trip to La Paz, Bolivia in South America, as it will show you why my dancing or public behavior affected me at a higher level. As I stated in Section I, Bolivia is one of the highest places in terms of altitude in the Western Hemisphere. The high level causes light-headedness and imbalance to those who are not used to that environment. Once I got there and adjusted to the environment, the high level did not affect me as much as when I first arrived. So once I felt like I had adjusted to this new level, I resumed my normal behaviors including dancing and joking around with my classmates. I brought my old practices to the new place (similar to many of you who are reading). I had the opportunity to go out with my classmates to check out the cultural scene of Bolivia and we had a chance to dance and experience Bolivian music and dance. There I was dancing away and having a good time with my classmates. But something happened to me.

Unbeknownst to me, I had something going on inside of me underneath the surface that I brought with me from the United States to Bolivia. When we returned to our living quarters, I became so sick that I could not even stand up. I was transported to the hospital and stayed there for almost a week. I found out that I had the flu and did not know it. I had something inside that came out because I brought an old way of being to a new level of experience! It is a true saying that what is inside of you must and will come out! Beloved, as you are moving towards your destiny and purpose, please keep in mind that you cannot transport your old ways (no matter how harmless or great you may feel/think it is) to the new level because it will bring things that are happening inside/in private/under the surface out to the public. When this thing comes out of you into the visible sphere, it affects your movement, your time, and your impact. I missed half of my intended learning experience that I paid my money to have because I was incapacitated by old practices.

You may be saying that if I did not have a latent sickness, then none of this would have happened and I would have been fine. That may be true, but it is this type of mindset that hinders so many people with great destiny and purpose from truly excelling. We all have things going on in our lives beneath the surface that we either are unaware of (blind spots) or choose to ignore (denial/avoidance/unrealistic rationalization). Ask yourself today; am I perhaps stifled and stagnant in my new level because I am bringing old practices to a new experience? Have I become my own hindrance because my actions are manifesting hidden, weird things inside me that now shut me down and slow me down?

New Wine in Old Wineskins

The Bible says in St. Matthew 9:17 NLT, *"And no one puts new wine into old wineskins. For the old skins would burst from the pressure, spilling the wine and ruining the skins. New wine is stored in new wineskins so that both are preserved."* I like how the text pointedly states that the reason new wine does not work inside of an old wineskin was because the pressure that comes from the expanding wine would be too much for the wineskin to accommodate. Wine has its own unique expansion range. Old wineskins were adjusted to accommodate the expansion rate of the original wine placed in it. When the Bible says you cannot pour new wine into old wineskins, it is metaphor. In terms of this book, the new wine is the room/platform/audience/moment you have been ushered into as a result of maximizing and operating with your God-given gift. The old wineskin in this discussion is your mentality before you came into the room. If you do not shift your mentality to prepare to handle the capacity of this new room, then you will stretch your mentality beyond its limits; and when your mentality is frustrated or shut down, your whole life will also shut down. If you are not mindful to shift your ground in a positive direction about your mentality, your viewpoint, your friends, your circle, your environment and handle them properly in the new place, then you are going to waste the wine and the wineskins.

Are you experiencing DOUBLE LOSS because you will not change your practices to fit the higher level? Years after this experience in Bolivia, I continued to dance but with a different mindset: I can dance but how, where, and with whom I dance had to change. You can do what you love and be yourself but you also must recognize ways to sharpen, improve, and adjust it so that you do not self-sabotage your destiny! Time is too short, my friend, to be stifled or rendered ineffective in this higher level. Be careful of how and where you "dance" at this next level because it WILL bring into manifestation what is lurking inside of you! You have to demonstrate with confidence that you have adopted a mentality that reflects the room you are in. I like to call this: "room mentality."

Room Conversation

As I stated earlier, each room, platform, opportunity has a culture, mentality, and practice associated it with. It is up to you to find out and know what that is before you get there; and be prepared to shift gears so you can operate maximally at that level the moment you step in the room. A major way you can demonstrate that you have room mentality is by your language. Using the appropriate lingo, exhibiting a confident command of the acronyms and a clear articulation of the mission are all factors that model you have a room mentality. Trust me when I tell you that all eyes are on you now that you are in the room! One of the things that some of the ones in the room will be doing is to see if you gained access to the room by merit or by favoritism. Do you have the training, education, skills, and experience to be there or did someone, who likes you, give you a chance in the room? Many of these people will never understand that it was God's grace at work through the working of your gifts and by the opening of the hearts of great people that gave you access to the room. Therefore, to avoid those types of conflicts, I strongly urge you to speak, act, and operate as someone who deserves to be there, and know what you are doing. Work your room, beloved! Otherwise, if you have moved into your room but have brought an outside-of-the-room mentality, demeanor, and speech into the room, you could very easily sabotage what you have worked years to build.

God has sent me to tell you that you should open up your eyes and recognize that you are in the room and you need to shift yourself to room mentality, room conversation, and room demeanor. For instance, in terms of being in the room with people of wealth and influence, you do not put your elbows on the table and be sucking your teeth and picking on your teeth when you are sitting at the table with millionaires that want to invest in your business. While you are out eating with people of influence and resources, you do not just order the most expensive things on the menu. Rather, you listen to how they order and then you order accordingly. Moreover, you do not eat all the food, which the Bible supports by saying in Proverbs 23:1-2 NKJV, *"When you sit down to eat with a ruler, Consider carefully what is before you; And put a knife to your throat. If you are a man given to appetite..."* Another room mentality point, in reference to the rich and wealthy, is that those who are rich often watch how you eat. They take people out to eat on purpose because research says people usually let down their guards when they put food to their mouth. So then, they want to see who you really are before they invest their money in your business, or before they attach their name and brand to you. If you do not recognize that you are in the room and you fail to keep the old and the new in proper perspective, then you are going to bust your moment.

PRINCIPLE 6

Preparation Starts before the Room, Not in the Room

I have recently been listening to people who are at the top of their game in various fields and one common theme I hear is that before they became recognized, famous, or successful, they were busy working and perfecting their craft. In fact, these persons had invested years of training, experience, and hard work before they ever became known. I guess the old saying, "Practice makes perfect" is true in this instance. Even more, while successful people were working and waiting for their moment, they often experienced failure, rejection, and struggle. Imagine going through all of these things for a hope, a dream, and a vision that seemed so far away and seemingly impossible in the face of so many challenges. But there is something deep inside of those destined and who are determined to be world changers. I am convinced the same thing is inside of you! I am here to help you mine it and manifest it through every part of your life.

The first step is believing in your dream so much that you can actually see yourself there, before you get there in reality! People who know that they are great can see themselves doing great things, being around great things, and getting connected to great people before it actually happens. As a result, they begin to talk, act, think, speak, and live as if they were already there. Believe it or not, practice will push you towards your goals much faster than you think. However, I am afraid that so many people do not have what President Obama calls, "the audacity of hope."

Let me ask you an honest question: Are you busy doing what you are called to do OR are you sitting around twirling your thumbs and pouting because your "moment" has not come yet? Have you allowed life's challenges and delays to discourage you from staying engaged in your purpose? The truth of the matter is that if you are waiting on your moment to come or for an opportunity to show what you can do, then you may not be fully ready for the next level. Perhaps that is why the "it" you are looking and waiting for has not happened yet! But TODAY is a turning point for you! You are being empowered to shift your mentality and adjust your perspective to align yourself with practices and habits that guarantee success. A while back, I was watching several artists being interviewed for an awards show on television. The news anchor stated, "This time last year, you were only watching this show but this year, you are actually here and maybe as a recipient of an award." This is major! Do not miss the significance of this statement. Your life can go from a place of dreaming to a place of reality seemingly overnight. Nevertheless, it requires work to cause the shift. The news personality went on to ask the artist, "What was the turning point?"

In the Scriptures, we find Apostle Paul encouraging his son in the ministry, Timothy to stay active in his purpose despite the challenges he was facing as a young pastor. Because of the obstacles Timothy was facing in his professional life, it was hard for him to stay focused on the great vision that Paul saw and prophesied concerning him. But Paul encouraged Timothy to do what he was born to do and to always be ready to do it—when you are on stage and when you are off stage. Do it when it is your season and do it when it is not your season! My friend, you cannot wait until your moment comes and then decide you are going to start getting ready. You have to find yourself active in your purpose every day. Treat each day as if you were on the BIG STAGE of your DESTINY! Find ways to make yourself stronger, sharper, and more distinct. Grapple courageously with your weaknesses and develop realistic strategies to overcome them. Set goals to get yourself closer to making your dreams a reality. If you are waiting on the moment to get busy, then you are NOT READY and the pressure of surviving in your purpose will overwhelm you. Be determined in your mind today that you will live each day as if you were already there. Tell yourself, "I will visualize myself at the top of my field/industry. I only speak and declare that I am there. I surround myself with people and opportunities that push me closer to my destiny daily." Destiny dwellers have seen/felt/visualized their moment YEARS BEFORE they actually got there. How about you?

Declare this proclamation with me:

> *Today, I declare and decree that I will am already great in my present moment. I am living, speaking, thinking, walking, and believing that what I am destined to be is already my current reality. I therefore commit myself today to engage in the things that will make me better, stronger, and more effective in my purpose and goals. I refuse to entertain procrastination, fear, and doubt; and I am determined, courageous, and hopeful. I am not a prisoner of my past and present but free to see and live in my purpose. I declare and decree that I already see myself*

*at my next level; and because of that, I am
already in the greatness of what I see. In the
name of the Lord Jesus, I pray. AMEN!*

One of the ways to prepare for your purpose is to anticipate obstacles and be prepared to address them. We have to view obstacles not as problems but as opportunities. It is true that man's extremities are but God's opportunity to work a miracle. One of my favorite biblical stories that demonstrate this is found in Numbers 27 about the Daughters of Zelophehad. I call it "Go Get Your Inheritance." This story takes place at the second numbering of the children of Israel right before they entered into the promise land. This was done to determine who would receive property. Well, there had been a rebellion before this point that was led by a man named Korah. He challenged and rebelled against Moses' authority; and God, in His anger, judged the man by allowing the ground to open and swallow him, together with his accomplices and their families. Zelophehad passed away but he was not a part of the rebellion of Korah. So when the leaders began to discuss how to share property and parcels of land among tribes and families, Zelophehad's daughters were overlooked because they were female. During this time, females born into families did not have the right to own property or have property passed down to them. Property was passed from men to men within a family. However, the five daughters of Zelophehad spoke up and claimed their inheritance, and God changed the rules to allow them gain their lot in the promise land.

Go Get Your Inheritance

One of the biggest hindrances to going on to get your inheritance is when you know where it is but have a situation (paralysis) that is preventing you from getting there on your own. Therefore, developing a strategy is of upmost importance.

Develop a Strategy

The first step is that you MUST HAVE A STRATEGY THAT CAN BE EXECUTED: In St. Mark 2:3 it says, *"They came unto Him (Jesus)."* This is a very short verse but it has a lot of background and history to it. A lot had to happen before "they" could actually get to where Jesus was. The man who was sick of palsy knew that he was sick and wanted to be healed and restored. He knew that the solution to his problem was with Jesus. However, he was immobile. So, this man had to get creative and strategic. He could have sat around complaining and whining about the fact that he had obstacles and blockages. Are you currently sitting in self-pity and depression because you feel helpless and stuck? It reminds me of the man at the pool of Bethesda who had been stuck there for over 30 years. Jesus asked him if he would be made whole. The man began to rattle off a list of excuses like, when the water is troubled, people get in ahead of me. Jesus asked him, "Will you be made whole?" not "What is blocking you?"

There is a saying I had to learn when I was becoming a member of my fraternity: Excuses are the tools of the incompetent, they build monuments of nothing, and build bridges to nowhere; and those who use them are of no use to the organization. I would also add that those who use them are of no use to the Kingdom of God. Despite the challenges and obstacles we face, we must have the faith to believe God to give us the strategies to overcome. If our ancestors had given up in the face of seemingly insurmountable obstacles, where would we be today? Many of our ancestors had little to nothing to work with, yet their faith and hope in God gave them the ability to take what they had and make it into something great!

There are three things that can help you develop a strategy that can actually be executed (Have you ever made a plan but it flopped on its face?). The first thing is to be clear about your destination. The paralytic man knew that Jesus was his destination. If your plan does not bring you to Jesus, then it will not prosper. Your plan will be aimless and scattered all over the place when you have no clear sense of where you are going. Be prayerful and discerning as you determine where you are headed. You do not have to have all of the details or know how everything is going to pan out but you MUST know where you are going. The second thing is to plan backwards. There is a planning strategy I learned while I was undergoing my pastoral residency—I learned how to start at the end of an event and work my way to its beginning. I would write down the anticipated tasks and then decide on who should be responsible for executing them, and what should be included in each task. When I started at the end and worked my way to the beginning, I would notice that I had overlooked some important steps and was able to fill in all the gaps. Perhaps, one reason why your plan is not moving you towards your inheritance is that it is not as airtight as you may think it is. There may be some holes and missed steps that you are overlooking. It is good to have people you trust and who are good at seeing/paying attention to little details and looking at your WRITTEN plan (yes, you have to put your strategy on PAPER). Fresh eyes can see things that your eyes will miss. Once you get your plan tight and well thought out, you move to the third step, which is to gather the necessary resources.

What are all the tools, people, information, and things you need to make your plan a reality? You have to be intentional, specific, and realistic when determining the resources you need. I am not saying that you do not use faith when deciding on your resources, but you must be practical and wise. Some people are paralyzed because they are not being honest and realistic about what is really needed to move forward. They want to use faith and God as a crutch or an excuse for sloppy planning and lazy work ethics. Yes, it is God that is going to give you the strategy and give you the grace to get to your inheritance but it is Him doing it THROUGH YOU or other people. BUT it is based upon what you already have in place. It is God working IN YOU both to will and to do His good pleasure. God is able to do exceedingly, abundantly above all we can ask or thing but it is ACCORDING TO THE POWER AT WORK IN US! Allow God's power to be at work in you to develop a solid, realistic, and practical strategy so you can get to Jesus and get your inheritance. I am praying that the God of all grace will grant unto you a solid strategy and give you the strength and desire to get busy towards making this strategy a reality!

Build a Support Team

The second principle to going on to get your inheritance is HAVING A SOLID SUPPORT SYSTEM! St. Mark tells us, "THEY" came unto Jesus bringing one sick of the palsy (See Mark 2:3). Well, the scripture does not tell us who "they" refers to, how many people were included in the "they," or the type of connection/relationship "they"—the individuals—had with the palsy. But what is clear from this text is that there was a group of people who supported the palsy enough to get involved in helping to make his dream a reality. This may be a challenging concept to embrace, considering how difficult it is sometimes to find people who will support you. It is hard to trust and depend on other people because sometimes folks are undependable, disloyal, secretively jealous of you, or lacking the things you need to accomplish what you need to get done. Have you had bad experiences working with people before? It leaves a nasty taste in your mouth.

One of my nephews recently had a tough learning experience. He is a nice young guy and very giving. One of the guys in his community befriended him. My nephew did not know a lot about him, they were really acquaintances. Well, the guy said he needed help moving some of his things but did not have the means to rent a U-Haul truck. My nephew, out of the goodness of his heart, decided to rent a U-Haul van for this guy. My nephew told him that he could only use it for a day and then turn it back in. The guy promised things to him. My nephew went out of town and while he was away, he found out that this guy had tricked him. He was riding around town in the van as if he owned it. He refused to return it to U-Haul. To make a long story short, the guy ended up crashing the van and ran away from the scene. My nephew was left to pick up the pieces. He told me, "Uncle, I will never trust anyone again. This guy has messed it up for everybody!" I told him, "You cannot live your life and never trust anyone again because to be successful in life, you need people." The famous quote says, "No Man is an Island!" The key is that you have to be more discerning and selective on who you trust. There are people out there who will sincerely and genuinely support you. You have to know and believe that God has assigned people to your life, vision, and dream. The challenge is being able to find them and be patient for them to appear.

This is absolutely paramount to building your support team. Perhaps, the reason why you are still stuck is, you have not allowed yourself to heal from past hurts and betrayals from people, especially those you really trusted, or you thought should have had your back the most. But you have to let it go and give it to the Lord and allow Him to handle it for you! By refusing to trust people and to be an "I can do it all by myself" type of person, you will position yourself to be stagnant and constantly running around in a circle. YOU WILL BE MAKING MOVEMENT WITH NO PROGRESSION! But I challenge you today to break the cycle and move forward in your life. I am not saying that what people have done to you was right or okay. I can imagine how painful it may have been. What I am saying is, take the pain and the learning experience and use it as the driving force to being more insightful and selective about who you trust and whom you will let into your inner space.

Protect Your Inner Space

Not everyone is your friend, and everyone does not deserve or need to be in your inner space. The "they" that brought the paralytic man to Jesus were inner circle people who believed in and supported this man so much that they were willing to lend to the palsy something that he did not have but needed. "They" were able to walk while the palsy was not! "They" were willing to lend their legs, mobility, strength, and time to help their friend get to Jesus. Your support team has to be invested in you enough that they do not just talk about helping you get to your destiny, but they must take action to make sure you get there! Do you have folks around you who do a lot of talking about helping you? They believe in you and want to help you but will never or seldom offer you or do things that will really help you. They may even have what you need to get to your next place but will not give it. Why this is the case, I do not know. But in this season, you have to open up your eyes and ears and take note of these things. While these types of people may truly believe in you, they cannot be in the "they" group! Keep these people close but not in your inner space. If you are trying to go and get your inheritance, you need people in your inner space that will talk faith with you but also do things that help you. You need people who are not just talking that talk but who are really taking action steps about that life!

Here is a vital thing to keep in mind: You need people in your inner circle who are similar to you yet different at the same time! Diversify your "they" group! The "they" in this passage had the same faith, work ethic, and vision as the palsy had. This is clear because they were able to come together to develop a STRATEGY (Point #1) and executed it well enough to actually get the palsy to where Jesus was. That took careful planning and teamwork. At the same time, I can imagine that this group was diverse. It may have been men and women, young and old, rich and poor, dark and light complexion, or from different tribes. We are not sure from the passage but what is clear from the passage is that they did differ in their physical ability. They were not ashamed of the palsy because he could not move. They were different from him. They did not need assistance moving from point A to point B. Is your inner circle all the same or just like you? You have to mix it up. Yes, your similarities are important because that is what often draws us to our inner circle friends. At the same time, they need to have some skill sets, experiences, and knowledge that you do not have.

I am pushing you today to take an honest look at your "they." You need to ask yourself some hard questions about them. Are they really for you? What have they done recently to demonstrate their support for you and your goals? Do you have a sense that they are jealous of you or want to see you fail? Do all your friends look, think, talk, and act like you? If you are really serious about going to get your inheritance, then carefully consider this "they" inventory and make the necessary adjustments. The first place you need to start is within yourself! What is in you that makes you bring people close even when they are not for you? What is from your past that causes you not to put a higher premium on your life? Why do you gravitate towards people who are only like you, maybe you are the biggest, smartest, or most financially stable person in the group? Why are you still holding on to the past? Why do you think you can do this by yourself? Be honest with yourself so that you can be honest with other people.

Be Creative and Determined

The third principle is to be creative and determined despite all obstacles you may come across. In St. Mark 2:4, the Bible says, *"And when they could not come nigh unto him for the press, they uncovered the roof where he was: and when they had broken it up..."* Can you imagine how "they" felt when they came all this way to bring the palsy to Jesus and they got there only to find that the place where Jesus was had so many people in the house such that there was no way to get the palsy inside! Some people would have become negative and pessimistic and given up. "All this hard work was for NOTHING!" But these people did not become discouraged. They saw this obstacle not as a challenge but an opportunity to be creative.

[116]

Often times, people get discouraged and easily swayed too fast—when they get to some crossroads on the journey. The truth is that if you are called to do anything great for God and the Kingdom, you are going to face obstacles and challenges. The enemy of our souls is not going to just step back and give you an easy pass. Satan will put blocks in your way to convince you that you will never reach your goal. But God also allows situations to arise in your path to see if you have the faith to press beyond what you see and tap into the power that comes from determined faith in God. Faith is truly the victory that overcomes the world!

When "they" got to the house and saw all these people, they came up with a strategy to get around the obstacle. You have to be able to think outside of the box, color outside of the lines, and move beyond boundaries to get to your inheritance. I am not referring to illegal or ungodly acts; I am talking about allowing the Holy Spirit to give you an insight into ways to maneuver around your challenges. One of my old bosses used to say, "When one door closes, another one will ALWAYS open!" Your task is to quickly identify where the other door is located and move towards it. This group of people who brought the palsy said, "If the main door is not the way to get inside, then we will make a door in a place where there is no people—THE ROOF, of course."

Can you visualize these people holstering the palsy up the side of the house without dropping him or hurting themselves! This required skill and teamwork! This is why you have to have the right support team around you. They got on top of the roof and broke it open. Now, in those days, the roof was made of clay and reed branches—nothing like the way our roofs are made today. This is a good point: While they got outside of the box by going to the roof, they also were knowledgeable enough to know what they could realistically do and could not do. They did not try to make a hole in the side of the house or dig into the ground. They knew the roof was easy to open up. When you are developing an alternate plan, choose something that you know you can accomplish. I challenge you today to make the determination that you will no longer allow challenges and obstacles deter or hinder you from going forward to get your inheritance. You are filled with CREATIVITY! Let that greatness inside of you rise so that you can have, be, and do all that God has purposed for your life. I believe in you and I am praying fervently for you! One area I am praying for you and of which I want you to be aware of as you continue to prepare for your room is your appetite.

Manage Your Appetite

I want you to be mindful and watchful of your appetite! That is right; I want you to know greatness can never be your portion permanently if you are not able to manage and subdue your appetite. When I say appetite, I am not only referring to food but I am referring to anything that you desire or feel that you need. That may be affection, affirmation, love, adventure/thrill, escape, or release. While appetite is as natural as breathing, one's inability to control it will grow from a simple desire to a necessity. When something becomes a necessity—whether good or bad—and you feel you cannot do without it, then you are susceptible to developing a habit or addiction from it. Your appetite is directly connected to what drives you and it dictate your behavior if not checked/managed through your mind. If you find yourself not being able to resist or give up something at any time for the sake of something greater, then you may have a problem.

When you find yourself putting at risk your destiny, hard work, and reputation for a brief moment of pleasure or fulfillment, then it is time to take note and get some help. Uncontrolled appetites will and have brought the most gifted, intelligent, anointed, and promising individuals from the top to the very bottom! The truth of the matter is one's ability to fulfil destiny is not an indication of one's ability to exercise self-control. Gifts come without repentance (meaning that the presence and operation of God-given gifts in one's life is not based upon one's moral condition). Oftentimes, addictions and uncontrollable desires are brewing behind the scenes of many great and promising people. When you hear of their scandal and fall, it is nothing new in our society! It is simply the public exposure of the long journey of these people—as to their moral failures behind closed doors. How many more people do you have to see or hear of their fall before you are awake enough to take an assessment of your state? Do not be fooled, thinking that you will not be like this one or that one. If you need help, then please go and get it! Feel free to email me and I will recommend to you resources and/or people who are trustworthy and can help. Your future is too great and your work is very important. Besides, at the end of the day, God is going to get His purpose accomplished in and through you. How you finish the journey depends on how you manage your appetite. Start strong and finish strong/well/whole/intact.

SECTION III

Engaging Great People

"and bringeth him before great men." (Psalm 18:16)

As a Senior Pastor, I strive to seek God for direction for the ministry each year and to develop a theme to keep us in sync with His instructions. This year, I was challenged and it was confirmed by my Bishop to focus on connecting Kingdom people to other people, to God, and to purpose. Usually, when we talk about connecting, some can have the tendency to focus on God first, then people and other things. But I challenged my congregants and others to really pay attention, beginning from this year and forward, to their natural everyday connections to the people around them. I really believe that if one does not connect with people sincerely and authentically, then their spirituality is in vain. Some people can talk to God all day long but will not talk to anybody in their house. And so you have some people who can pray a prayer through but they have no relationships. I would rather have good, open relationships and change the world than go in my prayer closet. So now, you have gained the world and have lost your soul with nobody to share it with.

One of the reasons this is important is that many Kingdom people have a good connection with God but lack solid, healthy, and productive relationships with people. Pastor Van Moody of The Worship Center in Birmingham, AL asserts in his book, The People Factor, that "clearly, relationships can make the difference between a great life and a miserable existence. They can launch us into heights of excellence and achievement we never dreamed possible, or they can keep us down in the dumps, tethered to mediocrity for all our days." Carla Harris, author of Expect to Win and managing director and senior client advisor at Morgan Stanley, is known in many of her speeches to say that everyone needs an advisor, mentor, and a sponsor in their aspirations. You need advisors from whom you can ask target questions and a mentor who sees the good and the bad side of you and helps you navigate the terrains of progress to land you in success. But she says you cannot make significant strides in your success without a sponsor. A sponsor is the one who knows the good and bad about you and can advocate for you behind closed doors to help you get to the next level! I want to emphasize that a major component to your success in this season is linked to you understanding the power of connection and investing in those relationships directly linked to destiny and purpose. God will use people, places, and things to put you into your destiny as long as you are working your primary/dominant gift that brought you into the room. The people that God may use to usher you further into purpose are great! Proverbs 18:16 NKJV states, "A man's gift makes room for him, and brings him before great men." The term great men, in the original language, suggests people of importance and distinction. Therefore, when you enter into the space of these people, you have to engage with them in a certain way in order to stay in your room and thrive in the room. This concept is important to embrace because many talented and gifted people place the majority of their attention and energy towards sharpening their gifts and working their room with excellence. While this is essential to success, it must be balanced with the development and healthy maintenance of the relationships that brought you to the career, opportunity, platform, or audience that has progressed you closer to your destiny.

Do Not Get Confused: Marketing vs. Relationships

One of the areas we can become overly-focused on our pursuit of success is in marketing or public relations. We can assume that our advancement solely hinges on the strategic

[123]

promotion of our stellar gift and the past results of using the said gift before the right audience and people. Yes! Marketing and promoting is vital to advancement but it should never take predominance over relationship! Remember Proverbs 18:16 did not say that marketing or promoting made room for you or brought you in front of great people. It said your gift! You get to the room because you are walking in your purpose and you understand the value of it!

Marketing only supports you working your gift in the presence of and with the assistance of great people. If you have a marketing team but are not working your gifts, you are never going to get into the room and as a result, you could potentially waste money that could be directed elsewhere. This sheds light on the competitive tactics some people use in their marketing ploys such as backstabbing and tearing down other people who may be on the same path with similar gifts. Listen, you will never promote you in a healthy, stable, and respectable way by using negative and underhanded techniques. Besides, you are a Kingdom person and you are governed by different ethics and morals.

Beware of Mishandling

Yes, Kingdom people are cut from a different cloth, so to speak. Therefore, we value the need to establish and support meaningful relationships. Doing so can make or break our growth and development in our careers, ministries, or ventures. However, I must state frankly that for some of us, in our intense effort to be great, we are perhaps mishandling the great people that God has brought across our way. The same people that you prayed, fasted, and believed God for could be the same ones you are mishandling. You may be asking, how am I mishandling them? One of the main ways people mishandle great people is by making them pay for the mistakes of people you met in your last season. You still have not been healed from past hurts, so now you have the tendency of taking it out on them as to what really belongs to the people who hurt you in the last season. I often tell the ministers that are under my tutelage to not miss their moments with what we have together because I do not expect them to mishandle our relationship by treating me badly, peradventure as they did to their former pastor, as though I have no value. I am not like him or her. I am not taking away from what the pastorate has done but I am not that person, and if they treat me like him or her, they are going to miss the assignment and the purpose that God has. Now, I must try to get them to see I am not that person and work with them because I can see their potential. However, if they continue to mishandle me, then they give me no choice but to move on from them.

Believe it or not, most great people operate from the same vantage point. They invited you into the room because they saw greatness in you and God moved on their heart to open the door. They will be patient with you because you are new in this space, level, and moment. At the same time, do not over-extend your grace with them by refusing to heal quickly from the pains and disappointments of yesterday. Allow God to heal you on the inside so that you are not in your room still feeling and looking deeply wounded on the inside. Otherwise, you can mess up your own moment and you may not even recognize that you are messing up your moment. Consider these great people as new opportunities that will help you examine what authentic friendship and partnerships are like. This face-to-face experience will provide you with insight and skills that are paramount to working your room. This may stretch some as we have moved away from physical interactions to virtual ones.

Divine Connections through Genuine Friendships

I think social media has been a great invention in the sense that it has connected the world in a much easier and cost-efficient way. However, in some ways, social media has minimized the space for real, face-to-face contact or connection with people. While many can boast about how many Facebook, Twitter, or Instagram "friends" and "followers" they have, I wonder how many friends can you call on the phone or set up time to see or have lunch with. Yes, be grateful for social media connections but make sure that you are building and maintaining genuine relationships with people. This is so important because divine connections and opportunities come often times through your real friendships and relationships.

I have been privileged to build some strong relationships within my professional and personal networks. I remember one time early in my law enforcement career, I went to visit one of my professional mentors, not because I wanted or needed anything; instead, I went because I felt an instinct telling me to go and say hi and have a chat with him. I texted him to see if he was in his office and he was. Because we had built and maintained a consistent relationship through phone calls, text messages, in person, and Facebook communications, I did not have to make an appointment. Otherwise, I would have to book an appointment with him because of his schedule and his rank in office. We chatted as we normally did about books, articles, the Scriptures, tactics, and life in general. By this point, we had established and built a good rhythm and we followed each other's flow. He said,

"Come walk with me down the hall." I did not ask any questions but simply said, "Yes sir," and followed him. I was able to follow without asking questions because I had a solid relationship with him and knew that when he did something, it had a purpose. We walked down the hall to an office to see someone but the person was not there. As we were walking back, we bumped into someone I needed to meet! This was the second time my mentor told me to walk down the hall with him and in walking back, we bumped into someone I needed to meet or talk to.

My purpose for seeing my mentor was not to see or talk to anyone but to maintain our friendship. The byproduct of nurturing our connection was that I had divine encounters with people I needed to be connected to. I share this to say that your divine connections and opportunities are directly linked to those with whom you have genuine relationships. You cannot build genuine relationships if you only call, text, and see them when you need something or have an emergency. You have to work to maintain real friendships. You cannot be connected to people because you think they will "hook you up" or because they are "movers and shakers." Movers and shakers know when leaches are attaching themselves for the wrong reasons. But when you are connected to people because there is a true commonality and bond, the byproduct of that connection is that doors will open, people will know your name, and opportunities will avail themselves at the right time. Perhaps you are stagnant and stuck right now because you have not developed or maintained genuine relationships through which God can open doors and connect you to the right people. Take time today to reach out to your real friends and let them know how much you appreciate them. In the words of Bishop TD Jakes, "The Kingdom is advanced amongst friends!" I just shared before that one of the ways we mishandle great people is by treating them as if they are the people of our past season. Another way we mishandle great people is by not keeping our word! Great people value people who can make promises and deliver. Unfortunately, we have a society of gifted people who will say one thing and then do another. Make sure to monitor yourself in this regard because not keeping your word can have long-term effects on your success.

Keeping Your Word

It used to be that a man or a woman's word was their BOND! In fact, at one point in history, people did not sign paper contracts on certain matters because people understood the power of giving their word. Today, unfortunately, people will make promises or commitments and abandon them just as fast as they gave it. It is so bad nowadays that it is even hard to believe people when they speak to you. It is a sad reality that many individuals live in constant suspicion of people's words and motives. Despite the fact that majority of people will not keep their word, those who seek to be world changers and successful MUST commit to being people of integrity. St. Matthew 5:33-37 suggests that a person's words should be so strong and true that there should be no need to secure your word by swearing.

> *Again, ye have heard that it hath been said by them of old time, Thou shalt not forswear thyself, but shalt perform unto the Lord thine oaths: But I say unto you, Swear not at all; neither by heaven; for it is God's throne: Nor by the earth; for it is his footstool: neither by Jerusalem; for it is the city of the great King.*

Neither shalt thou swear by thy head, because thou canst not make one hair white or black. But let your communication be, Yea, yea; Nay, nay: for whatsoever is more than these cometh of evil.

The practice of swearing means to make a promise or oath that you are going to do something or that your words are true. As a person of faith, others should be able to depend on your words because the God that lives inside of us is a faithful One whose words are dependable and true. This is easier said than done, I must admit. There have been times that I have given my word and meant to keep it; however, situations would arise that made keeping my word difficult. I would be tempted to abandon my word to take care of my own needs. However, there would be a voice inside of me saying, "KEEP YOUR WORD, THAT IS ALL YOU HAVE!" I would keep my word even if it meant that I would suffer or go in lack. Even in times that I did not keep my word, when I saw the person or spoke to them, I would not pretend as if I forgot what happened. I would immediately recognize my mistake and make an effort to make it right.

In this age that is known for the lack of integrity in keeping one's word, make a commitment to keep your word. The Bible says it is best to not make a vow/promise/commitment and break it. If you cannot do something, then be honest and say you cannot. However, people make promises and commitments because they feel they have to impress people, or over-perform for people's approval, or present this false integrity so that people will not discover upfront that you really lack integrity. The truth is that the real you is REVEALED when it is time to cash the check that your mouth writes. Are people constantly getting "insufficient funds" messages from the bank of your WORDS? World Changers are different from the masses. Start by being a person who makes promises they can keep, is honest and humble when they mess up, and works diligently to do what they have to do to keep their word even if they have to go in lack. God will always provide for those who keep their word, even if it is at the last minute.

Under-Promise and Overproduce

One of the challenges when working with people of influence and means is that they often encounter people who overpromise but under-produce. Why do people do this? I have heard some people blame others for why things have not happened in their lives. I am not fully persuaded by that. Hear me: I am not discounting the effects that other people's actions have had on you. It is very real and it is very true. What I am saying is that in many cases, the biggest opposition to most people's progression is themselves rather than other people! One of the main factors that causes people to hinder themselves is insecurities. Insecurities are thoughts, feelings, and beliefs about yourself where you feel like you are not good enough or do not measure up in some way. These feelings and thoughts leave people feeling open and vulnerable and as a result, they have to put up guards and facades in order to protect themselves. The problem with this is that it causes people to over-perform, overcompensate, and to be hypersensitive. When a person refuses to deal with their insecurities on a regular basis, the insecurities will often cancel out or stain opportunities and relationships that their gifts opened for them. I challenge you today to be honest with yourself, take a candid look at your insecurities, and come up with strategies to help you address them. It is not going to go away overnight but every time you attempt to address your insecurities, you are getting closer and closer to a healthier view of yourself, which is essential to moving forward in your life.

As a result, when people give their "word" to accomplish something or describe their abilities, great people can receive those words with guarded hopefulness. They want to hope and believe that you are actually the one who can deliver the "goods" by working the room they are about to give you access to; but then, that hope is guarded. They have heard "I can do this" or "you can count on me" more than they probably want to hear without getting what they were told. This is why keeping your word is vital to managing great people. It would be better not to make promises than to make them and break them. My journey has taught me that making promises that I could deliver effectively and consistently has not only opened doors but placed me in high demand.

Teachable Spirit

Anyone who has done any type of training or has been educated in a field knows that the more you learn, the more you realize that you do not know much at all. While the education process is designed to give you information, techniques, and theories, it should also give you a humble and grateful posture. However, many people who have been educated, especially at high levels, tend to lose this quality of being "teachable." Being teachable suggests that although you have knowledge, you are open to gaining more information, can handle constructive criticism, and can properly determine what you accept and what you kindly reject. Some people feel that because they have education, training, or certain

[131]

experiences, then they cannot be taught anything unless they feel that the person sharing information is on a certain level. I have learned on my journey that while some of my greatest teachers did have formal education, many of them did not have a college degree at all. A few did not even graduate from high school. However, they had wisdom, folk sense or common sense, and street-smart ingenuity; and my encounters with such people helped me navigate some tough terrains in life. As you go through your day, take an honest look inside and see if you are teachable or not?

Have you closed yourself off from great wisdom and insight you can gain from people of experience because you thought you knew it all or looked down on them? One indicator that you may not have a teachable spirit is that people in your field or workplace, who have been there longer than you, may have stopped sharing tips and insights with you. They may have pulled away because your posture was one of "I know this" or "I am going to do it my way." Another indicator that you may not be teachable is that the people you work with or lead now "fight" you. What I mean by fighting you is that they do not work with or cooperate with any of your programs, plans, and ideas.

Often times, this fight is not in your presence but subtle. Having a teachable spirit will encourage people to work with you and to help you avoid pitfalls that your education and training did not prepare you for. You do not have to be a "do-boy" or a "yes-woman" to gain this insight. You just have to be genuine in your approach, confident in what you know but humble enough to receive advice and correction from those who are more seasoned than you are.

Principles of Section III

Section III will explore Principles 7 and 8. Principle 7 is "Great People only Entertain Great People so Act like It!" This is so true beloved. If your gifts and personality were not great, then you would not have audience with great people. Although it can be intimidating and nerve-racking to be in a new place entertaining amazing people, you have to have the confidence and "swag" to properly manage these new and crucial relationships. Principle 8 is "Management of your Inner Life is Essential to Surviving the Politics Attached to Great People." While being connected to great people is amazing, it comes with some politics. There are people in the room with you that do not want you there nor do they want you to succeed. Great people often have blind spots or tunnel vision and overlook (by choice or by accident) some of the dynamics going on in the room. You can be sure that they are willing to invest in you and give you a chance to work your room. However, if you do not get a handle on your insecurities and other things, you will destroy your own moment.

PRINCIPLE 7

Great People only Entertain Great People, So Act like It

When you were a kid, did you have a hero or a superhero that you looked up to and admired? I had a few childhood heroes, mostly social leaders from the past who overcame major obstacles and challenges to do amazing things in the world. I am sure you had some as well, be it real life people or action heroes. As much as we may have admired our heroes from a distance because of their greatness, it can be quite daunting and downright fearful to actually meet and come face to face with your hero or someone of great stature. This is an aspect of success that many gifted people have not prepared for.

You have worked so hard to excel and advance by strengthening your gift, making the right connections, and executing your strategic plans. There have been distant role models and heroes who have inspired you to reach similar places in life. However, you did not prepare yourself to engage with great and influential people as your peers or close associates.

It is one thing to be a mentee or apprentice to someone great, but it is another set of dynamics when you are the colleague or the representative of a person of influence and means. When you reach this level, you cannot walk around acting as if you are an understudy or flunky. With that said, there is a code of honor and ethics that is at play as well. Your ability to land in the middle of being confident with great people yet respecting their position will be paramount to you working your room and experiencing longevity and success. Once you land in this place, you still have to pace yourself because this will be a new place for you that will require adjustments in every area of your life.

I Cannot Breathe at This Level or Can I?

When I was in Seminary, I had the opportunity to go on a trip to the country of Bolivia in South America for a few weeks with some classmates. As we were approaching the airport in La Paz, the capital, our professors told us that the city of La Paz was one of the highest places in this hemisphere. In fact, the altitude was so great that it would make us very lightheaded and off balance until we got accustomed to or adapted to this new level of height. I heard what they said but did not understand it until we got off the plane and I became instantly lightheaded and wobbly. While it was exciting to be in a new place and at a higher level, I had not taken into account the effects this would have on my body and my life. This is how many of you are, after you have moved to a higher level in your life. You are so excited that you are advancing and moving closer to your dreams and aspirations. However, along with this progression have come some challenges and experiences you were not ready for, and now it has thrown you off a little bit. You are trying to regain your balance and catch your breath!

The truth is, sometimes your gifts and your ambitions will take you to levels and heights that are so high and so big that you will find it difficult to breathe as you once did on your last level. When it becomes hard to breathe, then the body kicks into panic and crisis mode. You begin to gasp and fight for more air; your internal systems begin to prepare for a shutdown and survival mode. Are you in a shutdown mode and do not even know it? Let me share something with you that might help you. Once I got off the plane and noticed that my breathing was being challenged by this high level, I began to panic but my professor told me that I had to make an adjustment in my MIND and tell myself that I could function at this high level! As I made the internal declaration, "I CAN BREATHE AT THIS NEW LEVEL," I noticed that my body began to calm down and I began to take deeper breaths! Gradually, as I move into this new setting and allowed my body and mind to ADAPT to my new setting, my breathing adapted to the point that breathing at this new level was no longer FOREIGN, BUT THE NORM.

I know you may be gasping for air right now and feeling as if you cannot manage or survive at this new level, but allow me to encourage you that if you were not capable of being at this new level, then God would not have brought you there! God's divine power has given you everything you need for LIFE and GODLINESS (2 Peter 1:3). The key to unlocking it is to take control over your emotions and feelings and tell your mind. "I CAN BREATHE/FUNCTION/SURVIVE/THRIVE AT THIS NEW LEVEL!" Give yourself time to adjust to the new level by first acknowledging that you are not where you used to be! Embrace the new place by rejecting/abandoning/releasing the practices that gave you success in your last level and develop/observe/adapt new ways of being and function at this new level. If you continue to think, function, speak, and live on the new level like you did on the last level, then you will faint from lack of breath. But if you recognize that the breath of the Holy Spirit is with you to aid you to breathe at this new level, showing you new paths and modalities, then you will not only adjust to the new level, but you will THRIVE! One of the ways to ensure that you thrive at this next level is to make sure you are polished and prepared to interact on a consistent basis with people of influence.

Great People Are Polished People

One of my least favorite, daily activities while I was a recruit in the Police Academy was polishing my boots! I had learned how to shine shoes when I was a teenager but did not engage in the practice regularly. If I wanted my dress shoes shined, I would simply drop them off at a shoe shop. Nevertheless, my law enforcement training did not afford me that type of luxury. I had to polish and buff, then polish and buff some more every day! My boots had to be spit shined to the point I could almost see my face. We were inspected every morning during role call and if our boots were not polished enough, then there was a price to pay. The reason I did not like shining my shoes everyday was that it took a lot of work to get that initial shine as well as maintaining the final, brilliant look. Despite my fatigue, soreness, or busyness, I had to devote time to polishing my shoes. Well, the same concept applies to you as a gifted individual who has made it into your room in front of great people.

Great people are typically very polished and well put together. They have worked hard and consistently to be well dressed, groomed, spoken, and prepared for what they are doing. If they have invited you into the room, then that means you are polished or have the potential to be. When I say polished, I mean that you have the necessary qualities, appearance, demeanor, and grace to not only function in the room but to stand out in the room. The only things that should differ from you and those in the room are the amount of time you have been in the room and the uniqueness of your gifts and experience. But in terms of style, skill level, your articulation, or body of knowledge for your field, you should not come into the room subpar and behind the eight ball, so to speak. This means that you do not only have to know this level from book knowledge and research, but also you must know this level from some previous exposure. From this exposure, you begin to prepare yourself to match those who are not only in the room you are trying to reach but are excelling in that room. Then you will discover what to bring to the space that is distinct to your gifting, personality, and experiences once you make it to the room!

Otherwise, you may make it to your room without being fully prepared for it. You may be asking me, how can you make it to the room and not be prepared? One of the main ways is to have the talk of preparation without the actual substance of preparation. Without substance, you will be lackluster and a common person on your next level whereas you are destined to be brilliant and distinct in your room. For example, lack of preparation and polish will cause you to meet an investor who is interested in a joint venture opportunity with your type of business or venture, yet when you are asked to describe your venture in a couple of sentences, you are not able to do so. Moreover, when you are asked for a business card, you do not have one or the one you have is all bent up and dirty. These are signs that you may not be ready for the next room. For instance, you can be invited to a lunch meeting where your ideas on a topic are to be shared with some people of influence. Regardless of the measure of information given to you about the nature of the meeting, if you are like one of those polished people, you will always show up prepared to win and shine. Therefore, you have a presentation in your briefcase, on your tablet or somewhere to show that what you have to share is beyond some quick thoughts in your head but are clearly thought-out strategies. You are in your moment and you have to be ready to work your room, especially since someone of great means thought enough of your gift to bring you into the room. Therefore, go into that room polished, and stand before those people with a great poise showing you deserve to be there. Put your best foot forward in all that you do. Remember that all eyes are on you and you were built for this moment and opportunity so shine and produce at an excellent level.

Lessons from the Birds

Allow me to share some advice about how to engage and interact with great people considering that you too are a great person. I learned these principles by examining the lives of three distinctly different birds: the peacock, the eagle, and the chicken.

The Peacock Effect. The first bird worth looking at is the peacock. A peacock is a large pheasant known for its beautiful and extravagant array of colorful feathers that spread to more than 60 percent of its total body length. One of the things I have learned from the peacock in terms of the concept of engaging great people is that you must be humble but confident at the same time. The peacock does not walk around with his or her feathers displayed. The pheasant knows that he has a breath-taking spread of feathers behind him but does not have to show them to prove his greatness. As a gifted and polished person in the room, you must be confident that you have great skills, talents, information, and functionality but know when to display it and when to store it away. But at the right time, in the correct space and in front of the right people, you know how to release and unfold your greatness just like the amazing feathers of the peacock. Why is this important? While great people have invited you into the room because they see your greatness, they are still the one's who invited you in.

This means you have to remain humble enough not to outshine the one who invited you into the room yet be confident enough not to come across as one who is not sure that they should be in the room. It is a delicate balance you must maintain. Allow me to say it another way: when you are standing in front of great people, you have to know how to turn on the swagger/intellect/gift/input and how to turn it off. Sometimes, you talk too strong, too fast. Sometimes, you ask the wrong questions at the wrong time in front of the wrong audience. When engaging great people, you have to be keen on timing and location. Is now the time or not? Do you have enough discipline and self-control over your ego to bridle your tongue and not demonstrate your prowess if it means that you will upstage the one who opened the door for you? Even the disciples of Jesus understood that they should not ask him everything in pubic. In St. Matthew 17:19 and St. Mark 9:28, the disciples came to Jesus in private to ask why they had been unsuccessful in addressing the demonized boy brought to them by his father. This was done out of respect for their teacher and in recognition that the mentoring aspect of their relationship was not for public consumption.

The reality is that many of the great people whom God will use to open doors for you or usher you into your room have been wounded and disappointed by previous gifted people. They are guarded yet hopeful that you will be different somehow. People can have the tendency to ask great people for their stuff compared to finding out who they are and what they know. For instance, I have learned in my interaction with multi-millionaires that they typically do not want you asking them for their money; however, they are willing to share their experiences, principles, and strategies of success. This information comes through your sincere interest in what got them started in their field. Asking pointed questions about what got them interested and what directed their attention towards this particular area would usually open them up to share; and in sharing their insights, you will glean value knowledge. They want to be engaged because they are used to people asking them for stuff. They are not used to being asked about whom they are as a person aside from what makes them great. But if you are so busy spreading your feathers around trying to impress people that you are in the room instead of concealing your feathers until the right moment, you will potentially push away the very person who brought you in the room.

So you have to know when to come and when to stand back. You must learn quickly when to be seen and when to fall back because the person that is primarily seen is the person who invited you into the room. Therefore, you cannot be in the room competing with the great people God put you in front of because they are going to push you aside and now, you are going to miss your moment—if that ever happens. The person who invited you in the room wants you to shine and work your room. They will provide you with ample opportunities to do so but be wise like the peacock and know when to spread your feathers and when to conceal them.

The Eagle Principle. The second bird to consider in terms of engaging great people is the powerful eagle. Eagles are large and powerfully constructed birds known for flying high, preying on things that normally kill others, and having the ability to carry heavy things into high levels! I hope you caught all of what I have just said. Great people are like eagles in that they have achieved tremendous heights in their careers and endeavors. They have endured challenges and experiences that could have killed other people in the same field. The loads (i.e. family problems, personal struggles, setbacks) they have had to carry on their way up would have sunk the average person, yet they have soared to the top of their game. And it is because of these factors that eagles only fly and hang with eagles. In nature, you rarely see an eagle flying with a hawk, a chicken or a pheasant. It is true that birds of a feather do flock together. As a person who is engaging with great people in your room, you must remember that you too are an eagle. This means that you were built to excel and soar high. I know that one of my covenant graces in life is that whatever I touch or am a part of will not only prosper but also excel. You have to believe that for yourself too! You must know that even though you have gone through painful, embarrassing, and stressful things, it did not kill nor stop you from making it to the room. That means, any obstacles and opposition you face in the room is a light matter that you can conquer. In 1 Samuel 17:36, when David was being examined by King Saul regarding his ability to stand and fight the intimidating giant called Goliath, he said *"Your servant has killed both the lion and the bear, and this uncircumcised Philistine will be like one of them."* Truly, God will deliver you, beloved, out of any challenging thing that you might face in this room because of your track record with Him before now. But being an eagle also means that you will have to carry loads with you into the heights of your life. Being successful is not easy but it is manageable with the right strategies, information, team, and internal stability. I will talk more about this in Principle 8.

With that said, if you are an eagle who is surrounded by eagles, I want to lovingly but sharply encourage you to stop being around other eagles and acting like you are a chicken or any other thing. If you are in the presence of great people, that means you are great; therefore, resist the temptation to measure yourself—your personal worth—by how much you have in your bank account, the kind of car you drive, or the kind of house where you live. If this is how you usually measure your greatness, then you, perhaps, have missed the meaning of greatness. If you measure your success and effectiveness in ministry by how many people are sitting in your congregation each week, then you are overlooking all of the life-transforming things that are happening in the lives of those who listen to you. True greatness does produce results; in the same breath, greatness is not always about what you have on the outside. If you stay focused and work your room, the things you desire will come. This only happens when you place your focus on fulfilling purpose and not obtaining material possessions, fame, or status. Those are potential byproducts of destiny. It is about what God has put on the inside of you that you are working to fulfill your God-given purpose.

My eagle friend, go into your room and stand in front of the great people you now interact with and speak with confidence, not with cowardice because you deserved to be in the room. Yes sir, yes ma'am, I am here and here to stay! It is not about being arrogant or too strong in your approach but rather demonstrating that you are competent and equipped to work this room. When I engage, speak with, or present to great people, it is understood that this is an eagle speaking to eagles. I am not a chicken talking to an eagle! Why can I say that? Because I know that if I have made it into this room, that means that I know how to do what I do well. If I did not do it well, then I would not have been brought into the room. As a result, do not be scared but rather command the room!

Bye Chickens. The last bird for consideration in this discussion on engaging great people is the chicken. Chickens are a staple bird in our world's economy as there are more chickens in the world than any other type of bird or domesticated animal. As important as chickens are to society, they are limited in their abilities in terms of flying. Chickens are typically ground feeders unlike the eagle, which is a bird of prey that swoops down and picks up its food and then flies back to the sky—to a nest on a high mountain. I want to tell you that even though you are in a room of eagles, there are some chickens who are in eagle's feathers—they have snuck into the gathering of eagles. Some eagles have purposely allowed chickens to be in the room so they can execute their agendas. Your challenge as an eagle will be to say good-bye to the people in your life who cannot or refuse to go higher with you. In the same vein, you have to ignore the chickens who are in your room and are mad that you are in the room working it. Allow me to break this down extensively because this is what makes or breaks many gifted people in the room. It is not the great people or your lack of ability but it has to do with dragging people from your old season into your new season, even people whom you should have left there. Furthermore, it has something to do with your inability to ignore, maneuver around, and strategically debunk the chickens—both those in disguise and those in full chicken attire.

When you have been elevated to the level of an eagle, then you have to tell the chickens goodbye, which means that in order to be in front of great people, you have to manage loneliness. You have to manage not being liked by your old friends, colleagues, and yes, sometimes even your family members. You have to know how to cut off the dead weight because some of your biggest hindrances in your room are the people from your last season that you have tried to bring into the room but that person(s) either does not want a new level or does not have the capacity for the next level. You brought them out of loyalty, the kindness of your heart, or your ability to see potential in them. All of those reasons are noble and wonderful. It only works, however, when the person you have brought wants to be there and knows how to be exceptional in this room. Otherwise, they could become a liability to you and hinder you from focusing on important things in the room.

Sometimes, you have to let people you love, care about or have struggled with go! This does not mean that you do not love or appreciate them. It does mean that they cannot be in this room with you unless they really want it and are willing to do what is necessary (morally and ethically) to be prepared to work the room with you. If they are not willing to work hard to catch up and function well, then you cannot help them right now. You may have been carrying and supporting friends and family for five years and they have not gotten to the place of self-sufficiency yet. I only carry people that are committed to walking on their own once they are able to! Do not allow people to play on your emotions and kindness and thereby manipulate and deceive you into carrying them into your room only to drain you and potentially wreck your moment. I must be honest and tell you that this is easier said than done. If you are a Kingdom person, then you also have a heart and

[145]

emotions (callous and cold people do not act like true Kingdom people).

As a result, your ambition for success will drive you to manifest your gifts and thereby work your room but your heart will be sensitive to those who helped you progress in life and those who sacrificed to ensure you made it to your destiny. This is wonderful and should be a part of your being. What I am saying is that if those people who were there for you and sacrificed for you are not willing to progress and grow like you, then they cannot come into the room. You can still be in relationship and communication with them. However, you cannot include them in what you have going on, right now. That is why it is often said, for example, that you should avoid doing business with family or close friends because this is where the difference in mentality and work ethics becomes apparent. So if you make the decision that some people from your last season cannot be in the room with you, you have to be prepared to handle the push back and potential criticism you will receive. You have to be able to manage walking into a room that once greeted you with joy and now they look you up and down with contempt. You have to develop thick skin to those who always have an "I remember when" moment in an effort to manipulate you and try to make you feel guilt about your success, which may not involve them in the first place.

I Remember When…

When my brother and I were little boys, we were hellions on wheels! We were walking, little terrors and it was two of us! As you can imagine, my family had their hands full with us. But we were just over-active, very bright, and adventurous little boys. Now over thirty years later, by God's

[146]

grace, we have developed into prosperous and mature men. We are no longer the two little terrors we used to be; yet, some people like to constantly remind us of who we used to be. "I remember when you two did this and that!" I am sure you have people in your life who like to remind you of who you used to be and what you used to do! Sometimes, it can be frustrating because who you used to be is COMPLETELY different from who you are today. Even if you are still the same way you used to be, it is not ANYBODY'S business. Nonetheless, you may have shame about your old ways and find yourself feeling embarrassed when people bring it up, especially when you are around people who did not know you back then. I want to encourage you to embrace the "Remember When" moments with a smile. Do not be embarrassed or ashamed of your past because it was essential to developing you into the man/woman you are today.

Furthermore, do not get frustrated with people who constantly hit you with "I Remember When." Sometimes, people do that to you because they recognize that they do not know the "NEW YOU!" Because of that, they have no entry or access into your life. So in order to regain or maintain access, they bring the conversation back to where they used to have access. Some do this because they love you and want to stay connected but do not know how to do so with the new you. Others do it to try to belittle you because they are jealous of your progression. Many do it because your growth exposes their laziness, unwillingness, and/or inability to move forward with their lives. Your growth destroys their excuses for why they are still in the same place (physically, mentally, socially, financially, spiritually, relationally) you left them. If you continue to have shame about your "Remember Whens," then you give them access and control. But if you can smile and say, "Yes! I remember when" and tell the story better than they can tell it, then you maintain control over who gains access to you and where and how they enter. Never forget that the one who tells the story is the one who controls the show!

Ignore the Distractor Chickens in the Room

Similarly, you have to be able to walk into your room and ignore the glares and underhanded actions of the chickens in your room, who are trying to intimidate and drive you out of the space you occupy. This reality I know well as I am sure you do, too. For example, I have experienced tremendous favor and acceleration in my Marketplace assignment. As a result, I have been fortunate to be invited into some rooms that are beyond my age and tenure. I remember having an opportunity to be in a room doing something with people who had been doing it for decades. I was new at this particular task but had strong gifts and abilities. A great person brought me into the room, and I was working my room, too. However, there were some chickens in disguise as eagles, who could not stand the reality that I was there and were very vocal about me being there. The level of anger and jealousy I witnessed was mind blowing. But the great person who brought me into the room noticed these dynamics and pulled me aside to say, "You stay focused Dr. Jackson! You deserve to be in this room, so you ignore them and keep doing what you are doing." I share this to point out that although the chickens will be threatened by your presence in the room, the people that God used to open the door and invite you will never fall into the categories of such people. No one should be hard enough to push you out unless God wants to either build character in you or help you realize that it is time to leave a room because you are staying beyond your time. Overall, great people want you to be great and shine. It is the chickens in eagles' clothes—those pretending to be eagles—that you need to identify and watch; no matter what, just stay focused on working your room. You need to watch them because they usually plot on ways to uproot people from their room. If you are not careful, they can set you up when you do not have a clue on what is happening around you.

Beware of the Uprooters

A few years ago, I had a wonderful opportunity presented to me. I was able to work at a great institution led by an extraordinary leader. I was very young but was instantly granted access to the boardroom table and some of the inside operations of the organization. One of the people who had been a long time employee of the company instantly began to "befriend" me. This person seemed quite genuine and sincere as he began to "confide" in me about seemingly very personal things from his life. Due to the seemingly sincere presentation and transparency from this individual, I felt that I could reciprocate and share some things from my life as well. For me, if we are true friends, then I should be able to tell you sensitive and tough things and know that you can handle that information with care and keep it private. An important point here: just because someone confides in you does not mean you need to confide in him or her! Sometimes, it is a set up to learn your secrets so they can use it against you later!

Well, as the months progressed, my coworker began to tell me about the organization and the leaders. He shared the history and offered his constructive criticism. I did not know that I did not have the same "right" to criticize the organization because I was still relatively new. This information began to make me question the institution and if

I should still be there. It changed my outlook on the organization and some of the leaders. My coworker eventually had a life crisis, which was connected to how our supervisor at the time managed and tried to control our lives at and outside of work. My coworker/friend began to discuss what happened. As I listened, I shared my honest opinion about the matter and the supervisor in the form of a warning—"Be careful!" "Be watchful of this thing…" This person gave me a strange look and continued talking to me. A few minutes later, what I thought I said to a friend and coworker in confidence, eventually led to a terrible misunderstanding, and I ultimately left the organization.

Why did I share this story? I later found out that this coworker was strategically assigned to me to uproot me from my position by planting negative ideas and complaints about the organization in my head so that I would do something odd to either have me removed or quit. He was assigned to me because some of the 'higher ups' were intimidated by my presence and felt that I was going to take their place. I want to warn you today about UPROOTERS! These are people that pretend to be your friends, supporters, allies, and comrades, but they have a secret, ulterior motive, which is to hinder or stop your progression by convincing you on the sly that you need to leave where you are and go somewhere else—that is a tactic to UPROOT YOU. They try to make you think that where you are is not as GOOD or GREAT as you might think it is. Besides, they persuade you in an underhanded way that you do not or may not fit in with the culture of the organization. One quick way to spot an uprooter is the quickness to which they attach themselves to you and begin to open up. You may begin to believe that they are sociable as a natural friend maker. True friendship develops over time. Yes, you will meet people to whom you may instantly feel attracted but even then, it takes experiences and struggle to develop a bond wherein you can be transparent and real. Another indication is when they start dumping all the negative things, gossip, and their personal complaints about the company or organization. If it was so bad, then why are they still there? The reality is they do not want you there, so they are trying to run you down with negative things until you run away. Lastly, watch how they respond when you are working your room. If they have difficulty supporting you or celebrating you, then they are not for you!

Do not allow people to set you up to miss your destiny because you open up yourself too fast and allow folks to plant ideas in your head, which then cause you to act carelessly against a divine opportunity God has provided. BE WATCHFUL and SLOW TO OPEN UP!

PRINCIPLE 8

Management of Your Inner Life Is Essential to Surviving the Politics Attached to Great People

In Principle 7, we discussed that being in the room with great people comes with its challenges and stress. There are multi-layered politics you must learn to navigate smoothly in order to work your room. You are at a new level, in your moment with tons of dynamics to manage. You have people who want you to succeed in your purpose and you have people who want to see you fail and will plot to sabotage you. In order to manage all of these factors, you have to work diligently to have a stable, internal ecology. This means that your emotional, mental, and spiritual lives have to be healthy and intact. Let us be honest here: most highly gifted people are often wounded people. You have been through some painful experiences on the journey to success. Without these experiences, you would not be the tremendously gifted and stellar person you are. Nonetheless, when the lights are off and we leave the room to retreat to our home, the reality of the pain, struggles, and issues are waiting for us. It tries to wrap its hand around you in an attempt to squeeze the life that winning and success offered you.

I have seen in the Scriptures how God often times favors those who have been hated and wounded by endowing them with great gifts. One example that comes to mind is Leah, who was the eldest daughter of Laban and the first wife of Jacob. Jacob did not want Leah as his wife but preferred her younger sister, Rachel. However, Laban tricked Jacob into taking Leah as his first wife. Jacob did not hide the fact that he was not pleased with this situation. And because of Leah's condition of being hated and despised, God gifted her. Genesis 29:31 KJV states *"And when the Lord saw that Leah was hated, he opened her womb: but Rachel was barren."* God granted Leah the ability to produce children for Jacob but did not allow Rachel to be fruitful. I am a witness that God will cause you to be productive and fruitful in the midst of hatred and abuse. Nevertheless, you cannot stay in a condition of fruitfulness while feeling hated. You have to allow God to heal you inside through spiritual disciplines such as prayer and worship.

In addition, I strongly encourage going to a licensed and certified mental health professional for assistance. This is a challenge for some gifted Kingdom people to do because they want to spiritualize their situation or do not want to appear weak and unfaithful. Neither side will help you to have a healthy inner life. You need to couple your spiritual practices of healing with practical steps to get to a whole and restored place. This is important because whenever you make the decision to pursue your destiny and purpose, you should also anticipate chatter noise from people looking in from the outside and offering their opinions/criticism/doubts, plus those inside who are threatened by your presence. Therefore, you must be strong, resolved, and determined to work your room. This comes from maintaining a healthy internal life. As a result, you should not view people's criticism and snide remarks as an attack (this will be your natural feeling) but rather as a test to see if you are really committed to and confident in your destiny and to doing the hard work of inner healing. The reality is that it is much easier to stand on the sidelines and criticize than it is to get on the field and do the work. Besides, the sideliners make you sharper and tougher mentally. You have what it takes to fulfill your purpose; otherwise, you would not have been chosen to do it. Move with confidence that the One (Most High God) who selected you has also equipped you!

I share this information because you will face, on a regular basis, all sorts of distractions, haters, and dissenters and it can make you feel like you do not belong in your room with the people of greatness, who are assigned to move you forward. When this happens, you can begin to lose your breath, so to speak. You start questioning if you can actually survive at this level. I want to tell you that YES, you can survive and you will survive but you have to be aware of some internal practices that can hinder you as well as some strategies that can help you. Let us discuss the things to watch out for first such as procrastination.

Procrastination

Anybody who is working on becoming a better person can admit that the "P Monster" has held you hostage before. What am I talking about? PROCRASTINATION! Procrastination is by far one of a great person's worst enemies mainly because you can struggle with it in silence and come up with great, sounding excuses to cover it up. Also, most highly effective people often say that they seem to function well or supposedly better under the pressure that procrastination produces. While this may have some truth in it, allow me to submit that procrastination will ALWAYS prevent you from presenting the BEST YOU! You may have gotten on by the skin of your teeth and it came off great to everyone else but you know deep down inside that you are not bringing your "A game!" Procrastination is under-girded by at least three things: priority, fear, and pleasure.

We often times avoid the tasks that have higher priority and do things that can really wait until later but we do it first because we think it requires less energy or effort. The danger with this is that we push off and delay important things until the last moment and then rush to do it. The more time we invest over a space of time in our efforts, the more thorough and solid the product we have. Our inability to prioritize is connected to the fear of inadequacy! We procrastinate because we are afraid that we do not know what to do or that we do not have what it takes to do it right. We are afraid of people's criticism or rejection. We are afraid of having to defend or justify our behavior/words/work. We do not want to devote the time and creativity it requires to do it the way we know we are gifted to do it! So we avoid the pressure and fear by avoiding the task. Every time we avoid it, it weakens our ability to be tenacious and courageous. We have to take the bull by the horns and face difficult tasks head on and right on the spot, or else we will always run in the face of opposition.

When we run, we run directly to what is pleasurable! Procrastination teaches us to give in automatically to what feels, looks or seems good and to avoid what requires more work and effort than what we want to give! In order to be great, you have to practice delayed gratification and endurance. Today, make the decision that you are not going to put off for tomorrow what you can very well do today! Face your fears and oppositions head on. Put less important tasks at the bottom of your list and the most urgent things at the top. Trust God to give you the grace, strength, strategy, and creativity to do what you have set before you. The world is waiting on you to bring them the very best God has placed inside of you. Do not shortchange people because you are entangled with procrastination. On the other hand, you have to trust the timing of God in your journey even when it seems like time is not working in your favor.

You Still Have Time

It is amazing how fast time can go! Nothing demonstrates this like watching other people around you seemingly zoom past you in life. This can create stress, anxiety and discomfort within. But I want to tell you to take a deep breath. You are right on track with the timing of things for your journey. Do not allow other people around you in the room make you feel that you are less than they are. You may be saying, but how do I know I am on track or not? Ask yourself this question: What have you accomplished this year so far? You may have set some fitness goals, financial strategies, relationship enhancements, or spiritual growth plans at the beginning of the year. Have you taken an honest assessment on your progress, or are you caught up in the hustle and bustle of life? I ask you this because I do not want you to come to the end of another year and find yourself at the same place you were at the end of the previous year. However, the reality is that you may already be well aware that you have not met most of your goals. I want to encourage you not to get hopeless or upset. YOU STILL HAVE TIME to accomplish some of your goals if you get started now.

First, if you wrote down your goals somewhere, pull them out and figure out the factors that kept you from making progress. Perhaps you need some accountability or need to look at how you spend your time (time management). If you do not have your goals written down, then start there! Then prayerfully find someone who is successful at setting and accomplishing goals, who will talk you through your goals and hold you accountable. Once you write down your goals and the necessary steps to make your goal a reality, then you should include these steps into your daily/weekly/monthly schedule (DO YOU HAVE A SCHEDULE?) Your goals will not magically appear on your schedule and as a result, they will not happen. By placing your plan in your schedule, you put a timeline/time frame on your goals, which is absolutely essential to seeing results. This weekend, while you are running errands, spending time with loved ones, or handling business, take an hour to sit down and figure out where you are. And while you are figuring out what you are going to do, please make sure to place in your plans intentional periods of rest and relaxation.

Are You Scheduling Plug-Up Time?

If you are busy like me, then you can probably relate to always being on your cell phone or other electronic devices. For instance, I use my cell phone to make calls, Google information, read my Bible, chat with friends on Facebook, and do many other things. By virtue of the fact that I use my cell phone a lot, I have to charge it more than once during a 24-hour period. However, I get so busy sometimes that I am unable to charge the phone. This puts me at a disadvantage because without my phone being fully charged and functional, I cannot carry on with my normal activities. The reality is that I can only perform my duties at my best level when my equipment is fully charged. As a result, I have to be intentional and diligent to schedule periodic plug-up times so that my equipment is always ready to give out what I need to be successful. Just as my equipment functions this way, so also do you and I—as humans. We are constantly giving out of our intellect, resources, energy, gifts, and experiences at work, to our family and friends, and in basic interactions throughout the day. Every time you have an encounter, you are giving away a bit of your "charge." And as the day progresses, you can become depleted and close to empty. However, because you are so "busy," you can forget to schedule periodic plug-up times for yourself.

Stop and think for a second. Are you scheduling quality plug-up time for yourself? You make sure to plug your cell phone or tablet up every night or every morning to make sure you have it fully charged for your day. But what about for yourself?! If you keep going and going…giving and giving…doing and doing without replenishing your body, soul, and spirit, then you will tap out and become totally empty. When you get to a situation wherein you go to bed but wake up feeling more tired than when you went to sleep, then you are not scheduling enough plug-up time. When you feel like you are busy but are not getting the desired results, then you are not scheduling enough plug-up time. If you are being pulled in a thousand directions but have no clear sense of what or where you should be, then you are not scheduling enough plug-up time.

What is plug-up time? This deals with activities or actions that give you the energy and direction you need to advance in life and destiny. For me, it is my personal devotional time with God. I need this time to pray, worship, study the Scriptures, and encounter God's presence. While I know and desire to have quality personal time with God, I sometimes allow my busy schedule to shortchange my plug-up time. You know how you plug your cell phone up for 10 minutes…just enough to give it a little charge so you can run out of the house. Nevertheless, it is not fully charged and you continue to use it as if it is fully charged. The phone will eventually burn out. The same applies to your life! You cannot give yourself short bursts of charging! You must set quality time each day to charge your body (sleep and exercise), soul (reading and letting go of things that bother you), and spirit (prayer, meditation, and worship). Sometimes, you have to do it several times throughout the day—pray without ceasing. If not, then you will become exhausted, frustrated, and vulnerable to attack and misdirection. I encourage you to be as intentional about scheduling plug-up time for yourself as you are about your cell phone, laptop, or tablet.

You may be surprised what you can produce in your life on a daily basis if you are always on full charge. The result of not being fully charged is burn out and mental/emotional illness. This is becoming an increasing problem in our society. The number of people who are experiencing mental illness and emotional unhealthiness is exponential. I know that it has been documented that many of our most gifted people had some form of mental illness but that is not what I am talking about here. What I am focusing on are unwholesome conditions that present themselves as a result of not taking care of yourself. Preventable situations can get worse by neglect of oneself. If you are not well and healthy, how can you continue to work your room and execute God's purpose for your life with excellence? So sometimes, God has to help us get plugged up by pushing us into a season of solitude.

The Beauty of Solitude

Being successful is something that most people aspire to achieve in their careers, relationships, ventures, and life in general. Success is definitely worth working for and obtaining. However, success brings some things to one's life that are not seen or known. One of those things is solitude and aloneness. The saying is true, "It is lonely at the top." Notice that when you see an eagle, which epitomizes that highest level anyone could attain, it is usually alone, compared to other birds that are flying together in multitudes. While people invest their time, money, and energy into achieving their goals, they do not make adequate preparation for the "backside" of success. The reality is that the more successful and established you become, the fewer the people you can have in your inner circle. CAN YOU HANDLE THAT? Can you handle having to spend time all alone by yourself or to be extremely selective and cautious of whom you confide in or trust because sharing with the wrong person at the wrong time could cost you EVERYTHING?! While you are grinding to get to your set place, make sure that you have also begun to address what your need will be like—wanted, understood, valued, and surrounded by great people. Because "making it" in life could very well strip away all of those desires and realities. If you do not address and manage those desires, then success can do more harm to you than benefit. You will have reached your goal and be living the life but be miserable and prone to making risky and foolish decisions in order to meet personal needs.

Through all of your hard work and diligence in striving to reach your destiny, please consider the personal cost it will require. Learn now how to like having people with you and how to be discerning on who you let come close to you, for what reasons, and for how long. These practices will help ensure longevity in your destiny. Not only will embracing solitude help you experience success longer but also help you learn the way to access God's peace.

God's Peace

I have learned that next to God's presence, equity, and time, there is nothing more important in your day-to-day life than the PEACE of God! Life is filled with so many challenges, disappointments, and unexpected shifts, which test our faith and cause us to either hold on to the promises of God or question if they are really possible. Life's realities can really produce worry, fear, and doubt in your mind and heart. However, when we learn how to access the Peace of God, then it guards and shields us from worry and fear. Apostle Paul wrote in Philippians 4 that we should be careful or anxious for nothing. This is an essential principle we must embrace in order to operate in peace! Our response to life is not based upon what we see, hear, or feel but upon our belief that despite what we may be facing, God is our source and God is faithful to fulfill all that has been promised to us! It is that confidence that allows us to not worry or be nervous about any situation in life. Besides, as Jesus taught, what can worry add to your life that will be of benefit? The lifestyle of champions is one of radical faith and not ordinary sight and common knee jerk/emotional responses to what we see. Worry and doubt are the enemies of radical faith. Therefore, when you allow worry to consume you, you will become blinded to the possibilities of God being at work in what you consider a bad situation. Our limitations and extremities are but God's opportunity to do the impossible and break the rules—protocols and traditions—on your behalf. But it all starts with your mindset and belief! Are you worried and anxious about your life because of what you see or do not see OR are you living by faith and with confidence that all things and every situation you are facing is ultimately going to work out for your good? Let today set the pace for the rest of your week by declaring and decreeing, "I have full confidence in the promises and the word of God, and therefore, I refuse to be careful or anxious for anything. I walk in the full peace of God and I will move forward by faith to see the manifestation of what God has promised to me!"

Peace from the Practice of Prayer

Learning how to have peace is not about expecting everything to be good all the time. Anyone who is knowledgeable on the dynamics of this earth knows that life is filled with both the good and the bad—ups and downs. A peace-filled lifestyle is a recognition that regardless of my situation, God's peace keeps me calm, cool, and collected. The word peace in the Greek suggests, "May God keep you calm and stable in every situation." This definition does not promise smooth sailing all the time but instead promises that God will be with you and will never leave you. However, when you are in the storm of life and things seem to be falling apart, it is hard to hold on to this belief. Regardless of how much faith we may have, we are still human and governed by our senses. This is why developing and maintaining a lifestyle of prayer is essential to getting and keeping peace in your life. Apostle Paul says in Philippians 4, "That in everything by prayer and supplication make your request known." It suggests that there is no circumstance, challenge, or crisis too big or too small that you should not take to God in prayer. The hymn writer said, "What a friend we have in Jesus, ALL our sins and grief to bear. What a privilege to carry EVERYTHING to God in prayer."

Prayer is simply talking to God honestly about where you are and what you are going through. It does not have to be fancy or long; it just has to be honest, sincere, and

SPECIFIC! Maybe you are not experiencing God's peace because you are not consistent in honest, sincere, and specific prayer. Do you only talk to God when things are at its absolute worst and God is your LAST RESORT?! Or do you recognize daily that without communication with God, you cannot successfully make it through your day? Make prayer to God about EVERYTHING a daily practice and begin to notice how much peace you will have. Stop taking on the burden of your reality when Jesus has offered to take your burdens and yoke in place of His, which is much easier and lighter. We cast our cares and burdens on Him in prayer! Get to praying, beloved!

Labor in Prayer and Supplication

I have heard so many say, "Well, I prayed about it and nothing changed!" I am sure you have heard the same thing or have felt that way yourself. There is nothing worse than feeling as if there is no hope in the middle of chaos and problems. It is at these times that the enemy can begin to play with your mind to make you believe and feel that God does not care and that there is no hope for you. This is a lie and a trick. Allow me provide an important insight about prayer: Prayer is most effective when mixed with supplication. Apostle Paul states in Philippians 4 that in everything by prayer and supplication, you should make your request known unto God. It is not by accident that prayer in this instance also requires supplication. When you are in the midst of crisis and in need of strong help, you cannot just talk to God (prayer), you have to supplicate, too. Well, I am sure you are saying, what is SUPPLICATION? I am glad you asked!

Supplication means asking or begging for something earnestly and humbly. If prayer is talking to God, then supplication is begging and pleading. It is like the mother in

[163]

the courtroom begging the judge to have mercy on her son! When you are desperately in need of God's help and intervention, you cannot be all laid back and reserved with your request. Earnest means to be serious and sincerely passionate. When you are serious about something, you will commit yourself to it until you get what you requested. This may require spending much longer time in prayer than you planned. This means you may have to lay before God, fast, cry, shout out, and ask others to join you in prayer! WHATEVER IT TAKES LORD, I WILL DO IT UNTIL I GET AN ANSWER! That is the attitude of supplication. If you are detached and emotionless in your appeal, then you cannot truly expect to get the peace that comes in the midst of chaos.

You have to labor in prayer until God moves on your behalf. You have to pray and supplicate for several days, even weeks until God moves on your behalf. Supplication requires a commitment to stay in it until you get results. The other part of supplication is humbleness. Here, humility speaks of a posture, which says, "I know I do not deserve your help! I know that I am not worthy of your intervention, but I come to you because I know you are the only One who can make this right!" The Bible says that we can come humbly before the throne of grace that we may obtain mercy. You have to lower yourself and acknowledge your limitations and inability to handle the situation. You need GOD'S help and His help alone! It is this type of effectual, fervent prayers and supplication that availeth much—it is helpful, effective, and result-oriented. Today, I challenge you to "GO HARD IN THE PAINT" in prayer by adding supplication to it. You have to labor sincerely, passionately, continuously, and humbly until you get the release you need from God. Then and only then can you experience the peace of God when everything appears to be falling apart.

"Thank You" Goes a Long Way

As I get older and watch my peers and the generations coming up after me, I have noticed that people have stopped being polite and courteous. Basic things like "please" and "thank you" seem so far gone from our society. When I was a child, I was told that having manners and being polite would take me far in life. There is something about dealing with a person who expresses common courtesy to you. It makes you want to do a little more for them (well, some folks are too suspicious of everyone, thinking that others are only being nice to run the game on them—and, of course, some are). Thank you expresses gratitude and appreciation for something. When people do something for you, you demonstrate your appreciation because you recognize that they do not have to do anything nice for you. But I want to look at thanksgiving (the act of giving thanks) from a different perspective. The ability to give thanks comes from one's ability to THINK! The origin of the word THANKFUL comes from THINKFUL. The way a person expresses gratefulness and sincere appreciation is to stay in a posture of thought about where you have come from, what you have been through, and how this moment is so important to your next steps.

Thankfulness also exposes your level of trust and faith in the midst of tough, unfavorable situations. If you only express thanks when things are good and going your way, then you may have a selfish and short-sided view of your life. Why should everything always go right for you all the time? God sends rain on the just and the unjust alike. You ask "Why me?"

and I ask "Why NOT you?" The Bible tells us that we should give thanks to God in EVERYTHING (not for everything but in everything)! It goes on further to tell us that this is the will of God in Christ Jesus concerning us. So being able to give thanks in every situation, be it good or bad, is a part of God's will for our life. When we recognize that ALL things are working together for our good, then we can learn to thank God even when our natural response is to cry, be angry, or be depressed. Being able to say "God, I do not understand this situation but I THANK YOU!" opens the door to a level of peace and calmness that will overwhelm your mind. It is no wonder that Paul states in Philippians 4 that not only do you have to pray and supplicate but you have to also add THANKSGIVING! When you can think about the faithfulness of God in your life in the midst of a crisis, it gives you the ability to THANK God in advance for showing up in the middle of your circumstances and turning what appears to be odd in your favor! If God has done it before, then surely He can do it again! Your thanksgiving becomes a statement of faith and a declaration of gratefulness for all that has happened and for what is to come. Make a decision to include thanksgiving in your prayer and supplication. This three-fold combination will create such a strong bond around you that no attack or problem can shake you as the peace of the Almighty God comes into your situation and begins to work His power in your favor! Being able to say "THANK YOU" in the midst of your situation will go a long way in helping you experience the peace of God!

POSTLUDE

You Made It to the Room But Do Not Get Too Comfortable!

The whole thrust of this book has been about inspiring, coaching, and supporting you so that you can work your room and achieve the success that you were born to experience for God's glory and the advancement of the Kingdom. I pray that you have truly been blessed, equipped, and enriched through this book. I want to leave you with this final note of encouragement and instruction. Once you have made it to your room and have walked into great favor, resist the urge and temptation to settle and get comfortable in this room. The reason I say that is this room, while it may be great, is not your final stop or destination. Believe it or not, there is another floor with another room and if you get comfortable with and in this room, then you will never be able to reposition yourself to advance to the next room. This room is just one part of the overall journey. Remember I told you that many gifted people have to embrace the fact that their journey to success is built in phases and not in one lump sum. With this understanding, you then can see that there is not just one room on your trip to success but rather a purposeful and strategic string of rooms to which God guides you by His Spirit and wisdom.

As God allows you to enter each room, He gives you insight and cues into the length of time you are to be in this room. Then ask and seek Him for His guidance on what you are to learn in a particular room and what you are to accomplish while in this room. These three pieces of information will prove to be absolutely vital to your victory and acquisition in this room and your timely and smooth transition to your next room on the journey. Knowing the timing and objectives of the room will also help you not to become comfortable and settle for something that is good but not God's best. When Moses led the children of Israel out of Egypt, they spent their first couple of years at Mount Sinai.

Mount Sinai was a good place in that it provided them a closer glimpse into the workings of God. They received the Law from God, saw the physical manifestation of His presence, and began to receive established order and structure as a nation.

As great as the experience at Mount Sinai was, it was NOT Canaan the promised land. Their time in this room, so to speak, was only temporary and once the purpose had been fulfilled, God spoke to Moses and instructed him that it was time to move forward. My prayer for you is that while you may be in a good place in your current room, may you not lose sight of the promised place that God has ordained for you in life. Otherwise, you will set up residence and build houses and cities in places God only intended for you to pass through and pitch tents therein as your temporary abode along the way. Furthermore, when challenges arise in this room or temporary place, you can become frustrated and poisoned by the false supply or a true, past bondage. As many of the people of Israel were moving with Moses in the wilderness, they despised the struggle and process of progress to the point that they desired to go back to Egypt, which represented bondage and the old way characterized by a false sense of security and supply. Although Egypt was a place of oppression, the Israelites, at least, knew they would have food as expressed in Exodus 16:3, which states, *"And the children of Israel said unto them, Would to God we had died by the hand of the LORD in the land of Egypt, when we sat by the flesh pots, and when we did eat bread to the full; for ye have brought us forth into the wilderness, to kill this whole assembly with hunger."* Although Moses had a clear sense of the promised land, the people had not caught that vision. Are you a Moses with a clear sense that there will be struggle as well as several stops along the way until you reach your promised room or are you like the grumbling children of Israel, and you feel trapped in obnoxious nostalgia of yesteryear and what you used to have and what you used to do? Let yesterday's room be what it was and keep moving forward.

The inverse is just as important. Do not neglect or forsake your current room by over-focusing on your next move and next room. This is a sure way either to delay your progression or to make you a candidate to be recycled. When I was in the police academy, they had a system similar to the military wherein if a recruit did not successfully pass a class or one of our activities such as firearms or emergency vehicle driving, that recruit would be recycled. This meant that he/she would have to start over in many instances with the next class coming up. Sometimes, you are so focused on the next room or the end-point that you miss valuable lessons where you currently are and as a result, you can make some missteps that cause you to start over or have a delay in your current position. God is not punishing you but He wants to make sure you are strong and prepared for your next progression and for ultimate success. There are many rooms you will be allowed to enter and work. You have to know what kind of room you are in and then determine how you operate in it.

Landing, Launching, and Resting Place

I like to say that there are three places for great people: landing, launching, and resting places. Your landing place is that room where you found yourself at the beginning of your purpose journey. This place nurtured you, allowed you to make mistakes while you were in the room, and instilled tenacity, perseverance, and determination into your being. The landing place gives you the strength physically, mentally and spiritually to handle the stage of being thrown or launched to a higher level. This higher level is the launching place. For instance, this place is one where that final coat of polish is put on you by branding, marketing, social media, and exposure. This is the place where you encounter great people who see your potential and take the risk to bring you into the next level of experience and exposure. The launching place has all the necessary tools, resources, and connection to literally catapult you into the fullness of your greatness. Once the launching place assists you in taking off, then you arrive at your resting place.

The resting place is a place where you can put down some foundation and long-term investments and attachments because you will be in this room for a significant amount of time. Although we never truly "arrive" in the Kingdom of God, until eternity, the resting place is that "I made it" spot. The wisdom of progression lies in recognizing the kind of room or place you are in. I am sure that if you are reading this book, you are in either a landing or launching place. Therefore, I implore you to work this room you are in to the best of your ability, with the understanding that how you handle this room will determine if and when you will go to the next room on the next floor.

Prayer of Activation

> *Father, in Jesus' name, I speak and accept your words of promise over my life and being, and I ask that you help me to recognize that through my gifts, my eyes are open to see that I am in my appointed room. Give me the confidence to operate properly in front of great people. I pray God that you will cause me to never get comfortable, but always*

striving for more, always bettering myself, always studying, always learning so that I can continue to progress and go higher. I declare and pray this in the name of the Lord Jesus. Amen!

God bless you so much and again, thank you for taking this journey with me to learning how to work your room in order to find success in your purpose.

ABOUT THE AUTHOR

Dr. David E. Jackson is a man who knows first hand what it takes to overcome obstacles and challenges. God has allowed him to overcome various social and spiritual battles to emerge as a leading apostolic and prophetic voice in the 21st Century. A native of Atlanta, Georgia, Dr. Jackson is a highly sought after minister, presenter, and consultant throughout the United States, Africa, and the Caribbean with a kingdom mandate to empower people to discover their destiny.

Dr. Jackson currently serves as the 12th Senior Pastor of the Historic Mount Sinai Baptist Church in Atlanta, Georgia. He is one of the youngest pastors in the over 100-year history of the church. God has been gracious to the "Mount" as the active membership has increased significantly and rapidly coupled with the birthing of many new ministries and spiritual devotion to God marking this congregation as one of the fastest growing multigenerational urban congregations in the city. In addition to the numerical growth of the ministry, Dr. Jackson has lead the church in reconnecting with its history of community outreach through an active youth summer feeding program, Thanksgiving giveaway, and a back to school giveaway.

In addition to his leadership at the "Mount," he serves as the Campus Overseer at the Light of the World Christian Tabernacle Decatur in Decatur, GA, a new church plant that is powerful in teaching, worship and the prophetic. Dr. Jackson is a consecrated Bishop and serves on the Apostolic Council of the Light of the Word Interdenominational International Association under the leadership of Archbishop Ruth W. Smith. This fellowship is headquartered in Atlanta, GA and covers over 250,000 people in 13 nations.

Professionally, Dr. Jackson is a Community Liaison Police Officer, a member of the Chaplaincy Corp and a GA POST General Instructor at the Atlanta Police Department. His work at the Police Department centers around 21st Century Policing principles, Effective and Tactical Communication, and Mental Health Awareness. He is the founder of D.E. Jackson Enterprises, LLC, a ministry and consulting company that provides training on Church Security (The Watchman Project) and Church growth (The Pipeline). In the past, Dr. Jackson has worked in both politics and the non-profit sector. His previous work has afforded him extensive national and international travel including travel to over 15 nations.

Educationally, Dr. Jackson received his Bachelor of Arts from Cornell University (magna cum laude), his Master in Divinity from Union Theological Seminary of New York (Columbia University) and his Doctorate in Ministry from the New York Theological Seminary.

Dr. Jackson is a proud member of Alpha Phi Alpha Fraternity, Inc., Reeshonah Sofeem Christian Fraternity, Crisis Intervention Trainers International, Civitan International and the International Brotherhood of Police Officers. Dr. Jackson resides in Atlanta, GA.

CONTACT INFORMATION
Dr. David E. Jackson
D.E. Jackson Enterprises, LLC
3645 Marketplace Blvd, Ste. 130-266
East Point, GA 30344
404-969-5685
info@dejackson.org
www.dejackson.org

REFERENCES

Jakes, TD. "Power for Living." Shippensburg, PA: Destiny Image Publishers, Inc. 2009, p. 15.

Monroe, Myles. "The Fatherhood Principles: Priority, Position and the Role of the Male." New Kensington, PA: Whitaker House, 2000, p. 15.

Moody, Van, "The People Factor," Nashville: Nelson Books, 2014, p.xiv.

www.ingramcontent.com/pod-product-compliance
Lightning Source LLC
Chambersburg PA
CBHW061307110426
42742CB00012BA/2088